ROBSON GREEN
just the beginning

Robson Green has become a British institution. He first entered the public consciousness in the role of Jimmy the porter in the hit television series *Casualty*. This was swiftly followed by his highly popular portrayal of Dave Tucker in *Soldier Soldier*. The hit single that he subsequently released with fellow *Soldier Soldier* actor Jerome Flynn knocked Oasis off the number one slot and added pop star to his long list of credits. With lead roles in the recent TV dramas *Reckless* (which won Most Popular Drama at the National TV Awards), *Touching Evil* (which recently ran for a second series) and the forthcoming *Grafters*, the Special Recognition Award he recently won at the National TV Awards is a fitting tribute to his contribution so far.

Here in *Robson Green: Just the Beginning* the private side of Robson Green is revealed. His father was a fourth-generation miner but Robson decided early on not to follow in the family tradition; instead, at the age of seventeen, he started work as an apprentice draughtsman. After four years, to the surprise of many who knew him, Robson gave up his career in the Tyneside shipyard to concentrate on his first love, acting. Here, Robson speaks frankly about the reaction of his family to his decision, movingly about the love and inspiration provided by his grandmother, and openly about his reaction to the fame he has achieved.

This is the true story of the rise to fame of the north-east's best loved actor and with a glimpse of his plans for the future, this is *Just the Beginning* for Robson Green.

Deborah Holder, who worked on this book with Robson Green, is a freelance feature writer and author. Her articles have appeared in the *Guardian*, the *Independent*, *Marie Claire* and a range of other magazines. She specializes in relationships, law, social and sexual politics and is also the author of *Completely Frank: The Life of Frank Sinatra*. Deborah lives in London with her partner Joe and her two children Winnie and Charlie.

ROBSON GREEN

just the beginning

Robson Green with
Deborah Holder

B🌼XTREE

First published in hardback in Great Britain 1997 by Boxtree

This edition published 1998 by Boxtree
an imprint of Macmillan Publishers Ltd
25 Eccleston Place, London SW1W 9NF and Basingstoke

Associated companies throughout the world

ISBN 0 7522 1179 X

1 3 5 7 9 8 6 4 2

A CIP record for this book is available from the British Library.

Picture credits
BBC: pp 33, 41, 50, 51, 54, 55, 113, 114; BMG: 94; Coastal Productions/Brian Moody: front cover, 2, 37, 45, 63, 100, 101, 103, 104, 105, 115, 117, 118, 120, 121, 122, 123, 124, 125, 126, 128; Paul Cox: 77, 93; Phil Dodds: 96; Granada Television: 109; Live Theatre: 39, 47, 52; Keith Pattison: 35, 38, 70, 74, 75, 81, 85; John Rogers/Frank Spooner Pictures: 91, 106; United Film and Television Production: 99, 112; all other images from Robson Green's personal collection.

Designed by Bradbury and Williams
Designer: Bob Burroughs

Printed and bound in Italy by New Interlitho

Contents

Dedication

This book is dedicated to Alison and our dog Fern, my mam and dad, my brother and sisters David, Dawn and Joanna and all the rest of my family – they know who they are.

Acknowledgements

Thank you to Sandra, who made all this happen – as a result of this and many other things, I may now never have to busk on Piccadilly tube station, Deborah for all her help and patience, Johnny Geller for his support, John from Music Express, and not forgetting Pete, Carl, Zara and Michelle – what a great team. Thanks also to Joe Caffrey, Trevor Fox, Jerome Flynn, Patrick Robinson, Max Roberts, Tim Healy and Tom Hadaway and, last but not least, thanks to the whole team at Boxtree!

Fans wishing to join the official Robson Green fan club should write to the following address for details:

The Robson Green Official Fan Club
PO Box 603
Newcastle upon Tyne
NE99 1UB

I was four when the television arrived. It was 1968, over thirty years since the first signals had been beamed out from London's Alexandra Palace. But in Dudley, a mining village just outside Newcastle, televisions were still a rarity, and in Wansbeck Road we were one of the lucky few. It was only an old black and white set, passed on to us by my grandmother, but that didn't matter. For me, it was love at first sight.

Everything else paled in comparison and the novelty never wore off. On the contrary, with time its grip on me tightened. Television was a window on the world outside Dudley. A world of American gangsters, football, Ealing comedies and foreign films that promised a glimpse of

A BOX FULL OF DREAMS

something wicked. But most awe-inspiring, and one of my earliest memories, was the American moon landing of 1969.

We were allowed to stay up late, a treat usually reserved for Christmas in our house, and the excitement was palpable. With the exception of my dad – if it wasn't sport, he wasn't interested – everybody in the village was watching and half of them seemed to be gathered around our set. There was absolute silence when Neil Armstrong spoke proudly of the 'giant leap for mankind'. The newsreader quietly removed his glasses: unexpectedly moved by the significance of the event, he had begun to cry.

Americans said at the time it made them forget about unemployment, family problems, their day-to-day lives. In Dudley too, people were stupefied by the extraordinary sight of a man on the moon. We were watching history in the making and sharing the experience with millions of others across the world.

DAD TAKES US FOR A RIDE WHILE ON HOLIDAY AT SEAHOUSES, ON THE NORTHUMBERLAND COAST, A POPULAR FISHING VILLAGE THAT WE VISITED YEAR AFTER YEAR. DAVID'S ON THE LEFT, I'M ON THE RIGHT.

Television was a huge part of my life from that moment on. With the word out that the Greens had a telly, neighbours and family would often come over. It was a social event: there would be sweets and cups of tea, and my eldest sister, Dawn, would make sandwiches. There was a sense of occasion. As far as I was concerned, television was the greatest thing ever invented and, whatever was on, I lapped it up. I loved cartoons, like any kid, but was particularly taken with movies: everything from polished American comedies like *Some Like it Hot* and wonderful high-octane musicals like *West Side Story* to big, tear-jerking dramas like *It's a Wonderful Life*.

Television was the great escape: for me and the people around me. It reached out to the masses in a way no other medium had before or has since. And from those first fuzzy pictures of the moon landing I grasped very quickly the power of television to capture the imagination. To make people laugh, cry and think. To entertain. Given the kind of child I was, this power was irresistible.

I was born into a family of women: my mam, my nana and my sisters Dawn and Joanna, who were five and three when I came along. There were grandparents, aunts, uncles and my dad, of course, but it was with the women that I spent my growing-up years.

I was spoiled and that was the way I liked it. It was nature and nurture working in perfect harmony. I was a child with a lot of energy, all of which was channelled into making myself the centre of attention. On top of this I was a boy who had arrived after two girls and old traditions die hard. If my mam and dad had produced ten daughters they would have tried again for a son. I may not have been the eldest, but I was the eldest son, and it counted for a lot in a north-east mining community like Dudley.

My father wasn't at the delivery. It wasn't the done thing in those days, and for all his northern machismo he would never have coped with seeing someone he loved in pain. I was a seven-pounder and by all accounts not a bad birth. On the first day home from the hospital, Dawn came rushing home from school to see her new brother. Peering into the crib, she let out a shriek. 'But

Mam! He's black.' It would have made headline news in the *Chronicle* had it been true. In fact it was a combination of infant jaundice and the reflection from the red curtains drawn tightly across my mam's bedroom window.

The name on the crib was Gary, carefully chosen in advance and inscribed on the bedhead ready for my arrival. Once I was born, though, it didn't seem to fit and instead my parents let tradition lead the way. As so often in the local mining communities, I was given a family surname. Robson was my grandmother Sarah's maiden name, given to my father by his mother and in turn to me. Outside the north-east the name is a novelty, but I never saw it that way – there were two of us in my class at school – and anyway I liked it. Golightly, my middle name, is another matter. Borrowed from my great-uncle, a union leader involved in the Great Strike of 1926, the name is still detested in Dudley because he failed to support eight striking miners, who, had he spoken up, could have been saved from imprison-

ment. I tend to keep quiet about that one.

My mam says I was the worst crier, an attention-seeker from day one, and when my brother David came along two years later it was a terrible shock. My place in the scheme of things was suddenly under threat. One day this tiny thing appeared, muscled in on my territory and effortlessly stole the limelight.

I was mystified and a bit miffed by the effect he had on everyone. 'Eee, isn't he lovely,' they would coo endlessly. 'What a pretty boy.' Not being the bonniest of babies myself made this all the more upsetting – apparently I had a head to rival Humpty Dumpty.

But I wasn't one to give up without a fight. In fact I started as I meant to go on. A few hours after his arrival home from the hospital, everybody was gathered round the new baby doing the 'Eee, isn't he lovely' routine. By all accounts the toy tractor

PICNICKING NEXT TO THE HILLMAN HUNTER AT SEAHOUSES. FROM LEFT: MAM, ME, DAVID AND DAWN.

came from nowhere, with me at the controls, as I ploughed through the crowd and deliberately drove it straight over him. As the years went by I may have developed slightly more sophisticated ways of catching people's attention but the need to do it never went away. Every mannerism, the basis of my character, was formed in those early years and is still with me at thirty-two.

The world I lived in was small, with everyone close by. You couldn't move for family; my mam and dad's brothers and sisters and both sets of grandparents all lived within spitting distance. Anything beyond Gateshead might as well have been Australia and any dreams of moving farther afield came much later. At the time, what I could see around me was my future and as a child that was reassuring.

The village was surrounded by five coal mines, so the pit was always there in your face. It was the first thing you saw when you looked out the window and the last thing you saw before you went to sleep at night. All the men in the area worked there and came home at the end of the day with their faces still black with coal. If you could do anything else you weren't living in Dudley in the first place or you moved. Once the mines were closed it took no more than a few short years for grass to grow over the slopes. In little over a decade you could barely see that the pits had existed, but no one would have believed that then.

The miners were huge men, built like oaks, but the women were even stronger. They had to deal with the repercussions of that life: a husband coming home every night exhausted and often unhappy. As a kid I wondered what my dad actually did down there, but it was never discussed. He never spoke about it; no miner did, because it was a horrible job. Despite nostalgic stories of camaraderie and old-fashioned work ethics, there's nothing romantic about mining. Human beings weren't designed to go underground. It was the hardest of work, with little or no applause, and the conditions were grim.

Throughout my childhood we were always being told to be quiet because Dad was resting.

Dawn caught the worst of it. As the eldest she was supposed to be in charge of keeping the noise down, an impossible task for four small kids. Indoors we would play in our parents' old-fashioned wardrobes. One was a gypsy caravan, the other a circus with the clothes rail serving as a trapeze. There would be terror if we heard Dad stirring, because we knew we'd woken him. He was so big we'd hear the floorboards creaking as he came down the stairs. We knew that the creak of each step and the weight of his footfall as he stomped downstairs was a measure of how much trouble we were in. Outdoors there was little escape. The men came home exhausted from a night shift and took to their beds. The drawn curtains in bedroom windows up and down the street meant no shouting. Too young to stray far from home, we'd head outside to play football, but if we woke my dad there'd be murder.

At five I started at Dudley Primary School. Standing there in my new uniform, feeling scared about leaving my mam, I realized the world had just got a little bit bigger. Luckily my sisters had paved the way, and being Dawn and Joanna Green's little brother made the transition easier. Both were remembered as popular girls, good-looking with great singing voices. I was a little older before I understood that the lads who called at the house on the pretext of walking to school with me were actually trying to catch a glimpse of my sisters in their nighties.

After school we had the usual brother-sister relationship. Dawn, known behind her back as World War Two, was the boss and I was the most demanding of her charges. And if I was hers to torment, David was first in the firing line where I was concerned. With quietness a priority at home, as kids we were both pretty neurotic about loud noises and David had a particular phobia about clocks. I only had to whisper, 'Tick-tock, tick-tock' and it was enough to set him off, blubbering like a dog that's swallowed a wasp. If I was bored I could always use it to get a reaction.

We were expected to amuse ourselves, which was easy enough with four of us, but when the telly came it was a great babysitter. There was no breakfast television in those days, but after school, when Dawn was trying to get our tea ready, there would always be something on. I'd be glued to *Road Runner* or *Tom and Jerry*, and when she'd order us to the table I wouldn't budge. Faced with the ultimatum 'You either sit up with us or you go without', I'd go without.

The atmosphere at home was strict. My dad knew how easy it was to fall in with the wrong crowd, and after the tough times he and my mam had gone through he wanted what any parent wants: for his kids to move on to something better. Unfortunately for him, the most likely source of trouble lived only two doors away. There were four Hudson kids: two lads and two girls, the same as us. Living so close and having kids in common, Mam and Mrs Hudson became good friends and we'd often go over after Sunday dinner. They were great ones for a party and we were always first to be asked. Keith was the same age as me, and Colin a year younger, so knocking about together was inevitable. What Dad probably didn't realize was that we were far better off with the Hudsons as allies than enemies.

David and me, on the right, on the dodgems at Torquay.

My mam had two jobs, which wasn't unusual. That was how you paid the bills. She had stopped work until David and I started school, so she had some catching up to do. Her day job was in one of a small chain of local shops and in the evening she did cleaning work. If you were a cleaner it was kept quiet. I might not have understood why, but I knew it was something you didn't broadcast. If my dad was doing back shift – working through the night – she would have to take me and David on the bus with her. She cleaned in what seemed like the oddest houses. They weren't part of the local community – who in Dudley could afford a cleaner? – but tended to be in Gosforth, the posh end of Newcastle. It was an early insight into how the other half lived and even as a small child I was aware of a strict class division. I didn't want my mam cleaning other people's houses – any more than I wanted my dad going down a mine – but it was a question of economic necessity and it was only years later, when Dad's wages went up, that she could afford to pack it in.

Sunday mornings meant chapel. We weren't a particularly religious family, but it got us out of

NANA SARAH, MY BELOVED GRANDMOTHER

the way for a bit, so Mam and Dad could have a lie-in. We'd dress in our Sunday best for chapel and always got new outfits for Easter. There was a saying that if you didn't have something new on for Easter the birds would shit on you, so we'd all trot off to chapel proud as peacocks. Although I barely remember it, that's where we first performed to an audience outside the family. Dawn played guitar and we all sang. *Down By The Riverside* always went down well, followed by *Jesus Wants Me For A Sunbeam*. A lass called Leslie Aitken would try to join us but regularly burst into sobs from stage fright. Luckily I was on hand to console her – well worth the trouble because I fancied her sister, Karen. The chapel would also organize competitions, and we often won, with Dawn singing solo or as a duet with me or Joanna. As we got older we would also write and perform short plays, frequently carrying off prizes for those too.

After chapel we were packed off to Nana Sarah's for Sunday dinner: Dawn and Joanna one week; me and David the next. My mam's parents, Grandma and Grandad Meek, had both died when I was quite young. Grandad Meek had called the bingo at the over-sixties' club. It broke his heart when his wife, Jenny, died, and he died shortly after, when I was only six. So the grandparent we saw most of was Nana Sarah. Physically, she was tiny, but her personality was enormous. Frail and grey-haired, she looked like Red Riding Hood's granny, but she smoked like a trooper and didn't suffer fools gladly.

'Nana, you smoke too much,' I'd say.

'Shut up, lad – I'm nearly sixty-five.'

It made sense to me.

Nana Sarah was a gifted storyteller. She would sit us down and tell us wonderful tales of Africa, India, Australia, the Far East, or wherever took her fancy that day. Although she'd never left Newcastle herself, she'd heard stories of life abroad from my granddad Matt, who'd travelled the world as a soldier, and she was fascinated by what she'd picked up. There were no black faces where I grew up and her embrace of other cultures was unusual for a woman from a small-town, working-class background. I don't know where her liberal outlook came from, but

Nana Sarah passed it on to me. Along with that came a great respect for storytelling. It was entertainment at its most fundamental and a love of good stories has stayed with me. No one could tell a story like her. She would often say, 'I should have been on the stage, never mind you' and I suppose she would have made a good actress given half a chance.

A favourite was the goose story, which I would beg her to tell again and again. It was nearing Christmas, and Nana, a young woman at the time, had bought two geese from the market for Christmas dinner. The problem was getting them home; stuffed into a sack, their heads sticking out the top, they didn't take well to their first bus ride. Halfway home a passenger stood on one of the birds' feet and all hell broke loose. Feathers were flying and the geese were squawking fit to burst as they escaped the sack and attacked anything they could get their beaks round. I loved to picture the scene as she spoke: this tiny woman trying to force one hysterical goose to let go of some poor passenger's ankle while wrestling the other one back into the sack. When she finally got them home in one piece and proudly opened the sack to show my grandad his dinner, the birds took off for the back door, running for their lives through the streets of Dudley. It took Nana and Grandad the rest of the day to catch them. Come

David (left) and me on a boat ride around Torbay.

13

ME AND DAVID (RIGHT) SHOW OFF THE NEW *AVENGERS*-**STYLE MOTOR AT WATERSIDE CARAVAN SITE, TORQUAY.**

Christmas day, Nana didn't have the heart to kill them and they survived many Christmases to come as family pets. Nana Sarah also talked about the family, particularly my dad, giving me a sense of my parents as people and telling us things we would never have known otherwise.

My dad had left school at fifteen without much of an education and the pits were his only real option. His working life began at Seaton Burn Colliery, the same colliery his father had worked in before him. It was an old pit and conditions hadn't changed much over the decades.

What I learned from Sarah was that he had also been a ballroom dancer until he was twenty-one, rising to semi-professional status and triumphing as waltz champion of the north-east. With his sister Brenda as his dancing partner, he toured the country, competing in tournaments and appearing in exhibitions. They were so well known, Sarah told us proudly, that local people from Dudley took bus trips to see them perform.

Her favourite story, though, was of the night Brenda and my dad were tipped to win a prestigious dancing competition. When their names were announced, the crowd buzzed with anticipation, the curtains swept back and there was Brenda, in her yellow tutu and my dad in top and tails, knocking

seven bells out of each other. The organizers had to separate them and the two were disqualified.

Dad and Mam had married soon after meeting and it wasn't long before Mam was pregnant with Dawn. She gave up her job as a secretary and Dad stopped dancing. The subject was a closed book by the time we came along and, as a man who tends not to look back, he never mentioned it.

Perhaps he thought it wasn't fair to carry on dancing. Life had changed, become more serious. He was a married man and about to become a father. As a semi-professional dancer, he needed to be away from home a lot and practice demanded most of the little spare time he had between the pit and his bed.

It's also possible that the person with the real yen for show business was Nana Sarah. For my dad, dancing began as a hobby, something he now says he enjoyed but never intended to pursue. For Sarah, it opened the door to the exciting and glamorous world of exotic costumes, music, lights and applause. After the war, she told us, shows were held to raise money for the soldiers who had come back injured and Dad, who was working in the pits by day, would save up his days off for performances. He and Auntie Brenda would dance and Sarah would always travel with them to help behind the scenes. It must have been a shock for her when the show suddenly stopped, particularly as Dad and Brenda had just qualified to teach and she may have seen the possibility of a career in entertainment for the two of them.

For Dad, as a third-generation miner, it was probably all too much of a risk and in any case it would hardly have been considered a suitable job for a man. He maintains he never regretted it and was quite happy to give it up when he did. Years later he would still take to the floor at the Fusilier when the mood took him, and from the age of seven or eight I would sometimes hear his great, boomy voice echoing out of local pubs and working men's clubs. We would always have to wait outside, of course, but we'd catch snatches of *Leaving On A Jet Plane*, Elvis and Buddy Holly classics and one of his favourite ballads, *I Believe*. Dad was still a showman at heart, but as a miner and father of four, it was only ever a bit of fun after that.

CHAPTER TWO

David and I shared a bedroom. The view from our window was the curve of Seaton Burn, with the moors stretching away into the distance beyond. The burn was a gathering point for kids, but with Dad being stricter than most we were always sent to bed early. While they'd be playing on rafts, laughing and messing around, we'd be inside, looking out. It was well-meant concern on my parents' part, but it was tough on me and David, especially in the summer months, when the days were long. We'd be penned in upstairs, daylight still pouring through the window, listening to the other kids laughing, playing. Keith and Colin Hudson were allowed out, of course, and they'd sit beside the fence shouting up to us as if we

THE EARLY YEARS

and he knew it. If he said 'Sit' we sat and if he smacked you, you felt it. If I was playing up he'd always have one of his favourite lines at the ready: 'I'll make you smile on the other side of your face' or 'There's a lot more where that came from.' They were meant to scare me, but instead I used to crack up at the nonsensical things adults came up with when they were mad.

He wasn't a violent man but he believed in discipline and I was aware of his strength, which, as long as I wasn't in the firing line, had its advantages. When I was a bit older a kid from a local gang kicked our David; we were playing football and some lads came from the next village, tried to nick the ball and booted my brother in the process. Dad saw what was happening from the bedroom window and came thundering down in only his vest and braces. This lad was pretty big, but my dad just brushed him off with one hand and he shifted about twenty yards.

were prisoners. It was embarrassing as much as anything else and we'd sometimes get teased about it at school.

To relieve the boredom we worked out a system for watching television from the top of the stairs. There was a mirror in the toilet and if we got the angle just right we could watch an inverted image beamed up from the living room and reflected in the mirror. I remember perching on the top stair with David, both in pyjamas, stifling laughter as we secretly watched a reflected John Cleese trying to beat his Mini into action. I was addicted and even just listening was sometimes enough.

I was a very skinny kid, small and slightly built; my dad always said I'd make a good jockey. I certainly didn't seem to take after him. When I was six or seven he was knocking on nineteen stone. He was a solid guy, the hardest in the village, and that was a big thing. I was scared of him as a child

As a kid I quite liked it because I always felt safe. Dad used to take us to the Hopping's, the biggest fair in Europe, and I felt very secure in the middle of the heaving crowd with my hand in his. Later on, despite a fairly authoritarian upbringing, I didn't go through the rebellious stage that might have been expected when my parents divorced and Dad was no longer living at home. The truth is, I liked the security that came with the firm hand.

Being small at school could have been a problem, especially as I was one of the only boys interested in music and drama – subjects traditionally seen as strictly for girls or sissies. But the solution for me was to talk my way out of trouble. If I could make a potential bully laugh I could usually escape a thrashing.

My first experiences of live entertainment were football matches and panto. When we saw *Aladdin* at Newcastle's Theatre Royal, the exuberance of the audience was a revelation. It was a big, brash spectacle: men dressed as women screamed out to the kids and threw sweets into the crowd, costume changes came fast and furious and a genie appeared in a cloud of smoke. Best of all, the rowdy feedback from the audience was immediate and unchecked. I was hooked and I wanted to be on the receiving end.

Encouragement came from Miss Anderson, my music teacher at Dudley Primary. She was attrac-tive, could sing and play guitar and I probably had a bit of a crush on her. If there was a nativity play or school concert, I was always first in the line. My first starring role was the lead in *Joseph and His Amazing Technicolor Dreamcoat*. I'd actually fancied the Pharaoh's part – he had all the best songs and got all the laughs – but I don't think Miss Anderson thought I had it in me to be big and bad enough.

Unfortunately, teachers like Miss Anderson were an exception. The general

LARKING ABOUT ON THE BEACH WITH DAVID IN TORQUAY.

approach was education by fear and the head-master, Mr Jones, was the most terrifying of all. Always immaculately dressed, with small, round glasses and a neat, bald head, he would tower over us in assembly, rocking back and forth on the balls of his feet. Standing quaking outside his office waiting for the strap was a regular occurrence for plenty of kids and a frightening enough prospect to keep the rest of us in line. I caught the odd smack but managed to escape the strap. Others weren't as lucky. When one lad was strapped in front of the whole school at assembly I found it hard to understand what he could have done to deserve such a violent and humiliating punishment.

Mam always came to see me in all my school plays from primary school on. I enjoyed being centre stage so much that I was totally fearless just as Mam described Dad in his dancing days: fearless and competitive, a perfectionist never content with second place. Mam will tell me now how Dad and Brenda practised for hours, giving it absolute concentration, and that's how I approached acting even as a kid.

While I didn't dislike school, I didn't take it seriously either. My reports always read the same: 'Robson Green is easily distracted and easily distracts others.' If it was hard to hold my attention in class, outside school I was never bored and always looking for things to do. We had a little cassette tape recorder and I would make tapes of impressions I'd perfected as well as little plays I'd written. My main preoccupations, though, were still telly, and now football.

Football was a huge part of our lives whether it was playing or going to games with my dad, who had been quite a player in his youth. In working communities on Tyneside it was an escape from the mundane life men were leading in industry, the one day in the week they could get away and find some sort of release. It also gave people a great sense of pride; when your team was doing well you felt good about yourself.

For working-class men it was also the only acceptable outlet for uninhibited emotional expression, and I saw that in my dad and his

BELOW: LEFT TO RIGHT: HELEN JEFFRIES, ME, JOANNA, DAD AND DAVID AT A THEME PARK IN TORBAY. BELOW RIGHT: HELEN, DAVID, ME, JOANNA AND DAD ON THE SAME HOLIDAY.

mates. He may not have talked a lot but, like me, sport would make him very emotional. A live match really puts you through it, from hysterical elation to anger and despair. It's an occasion, a great dramatic event and as close as many working-class people get to theatre. On a practical level it was also one of the few escape routes alongside entertainment, but not one I was ever good enough to pursue as much as I would have liked to.

I was seven when my dad took me to my first match. It was Newcastle versus West Ham and I went with Dad and his three mates – Albie, Plum and Mickey – on their season tickets. Newcastle won 3–2 but I wasn't as interested in the game as in watching the crowd. It was organized chaos. There were little fights breaking out in the Leazes end, people pinching coppers' hats and throwing them to each other, a huge outpouring of mass emotion. It was also the first time I heard Dad say the F-word. Everybody was swaying, singing and chanting; it was impossible to hear the words, but everybody seemed to know them, as if there were secret classes going on somewhere.

AT WATERSIDE CARAVAN PARK, TORQUAY, DAVID AND I SHOW OFF OUR ONLY CATCH AFTER A FIVE-HOUR BOAT TRIP WITH DAD.

I hadn't seen Newcastle play in their glory days. Historically we were at our strongest in the fifties. We were the Man U of our day and Dad often reminisced about heroes like Jackie Milburn and Hughie Gallacher at their peak. Years later, when Milburn died, the streets of Newcastle came to a standstill. Grown men wept and the few who didn't

LEFT TO RIGHT: DAVID, ME, JOANNA'S FRIEND MAUREEN AND JOANNA IN SPAIN.

around at his spellbound schoolboy audience and chatted about his plans at Newcastle, I could barely take it in. Then, with a glance at my half-eaten plate of sausages, mash and peas, he said, 'You better eat those peas, lad. They're good for you.' Well, he might as well have let me in on the meaning of life itself. I couldn't get home fast enough that day. 'Dad, he said: "Eat your peas." That's what he said, Dad: "EAT YOUR PEAS"!'

Football also provided one of my greatest disappointments. In 1974 Newcastle were due to take on Liverpool at

know football couldn't understand what was happening. I had to wait for another legend to come along to change everything for Newcastle.

Malcolm MacDonald, 'Supermac', was the man to do it. It was a career cut short by injury, but what a career it was while it lasted. He was a great sprinter and nobody could touch him. Running on to a pass, usually from Terry Hibbert, he would head for goal. He moved like a gazelle and there was huge expectancy when he stepped on to the field. Yet even that was nothing to touch the excitement when he came to visit my school.

When Mr Jones interrupted lunch to announce that we had a special guest we had no idea who to expect. Supermac, it turned out, was in the area to open a local business and one of the teachers had run across the road and asked him to come in and say hello to the kids. All of a sudden there he was. It was my hero walking through the double doors and heading in my direction. And to my amazement, he just kept coming, skirting through the islands of dinner tables, shaking hands as he approached and with four hundred kids to choose from, he sat down right between me and Colin Hudson. For once I was speechless. As he looked

Wembley. It was the FA Cup Final, they had Keegan and it promised to be a cracking game. When the big day arrived David and I were up with the birds, dressed and ready for the airport before anyone else had stirred in their beds: black and white shirts and scarves, big pom-pom hats, flags – the lot. We piled into the car too excited to ask questions and it was only when Mam started to explain that Dad was going to park the car and we were going to get a taxi back that it slowly began to sink in. We weren't going anywhere. Too young to understand air fares and ticket availability, the thought hadn't crossed our minds until that moment. There we were, looking like a couple of penguins, dressed to the nines in black and white gear, and the next thing we knew we were waving him off at the airport.

It was tragic and things went from bad to worse as we started to lose. David, Keith Hudson and I ended up sitting outside, near the Burn, still in our gear, Magpie banner in hand, half-heartedly munching crisps and listening to the tragedy unfold on a battered old transistor radio. We'd started off watching it on telly but it was unbearable to see in such merciless detail. As it turned out, Dad left the stadium before the final whistle too – something he'd never done before. We got slaughtered 3–0.

When the nearest Dudley pit closed in the seventies I didn't really understand the significance for the community. My dad moved to another pit, in Ellington, as a deputy and stayed there until that too closed in the 1984 strike. So for him, ironically, the closure meant slightly better conditions and a better job. For me, the overriding memory is the appearance of the pit ponies. No longer needed, they were brought up and put to grass around the pit after a lifetime of hauling tubs of coal along the railway lines and bringing it up from the mine. They'd rarely seen the light of day because once they were above ground it was too difficult to get them down again. The men would push the tubs from behind and

GIRLS, GALAS' AND MORE GIRLS

pull from up front, with the ponies in the middle. Dad had started as a puller before going on to become a face worker.

The ponies had spent a life in blinkers and some went crazy when they finally came to the surface. Oblivious to the fact that they were only there while waiting to be destroyed, the local kids used to feed and ride them. Some were taken as pets and a piebald we called Billy became my favourite. A few months later they disappeared as suddenly as they had arrived.

With Dad in a new job there was a bit more cash available for extras. A lot of it went towards family holidays, but with four kids to shell out for we were usually limited to country caravan sites, like Seahouses, in Northumberland, or B&Bs near the Devon coast.

It was fine once we arrived but the nine-hour journey to Devon with six of us plus luggage packed into the Hillman Hunter was not something we looked forward to. Crawling down the motorway with my parents arguing about my mam's failings as a navigator, it felt like we were setting off to Australia. Dad had a short fuse and if it wasn't Mam's directions that set him off, it was us bickering too loudly in the back.

As soon as we'd settled in you wouldn't see my sisters for dust: they'd be off in search of boys the minute we finished unpacking. Too young to escape, David and I would hang about the river, sometimes going boat fishing with my dad, but we had to be home in the caravan at six o'clock sharp every evening.

One of the best holidays was a fortnight in Devon which included a trip to see the Red Devils. Standing in the crowd, we held our breath as parachutists in their trademark red jump suits plunged from roaring planes and descended in formation, explosive coloured flares streaming from their heels. To an eight-year-old boy these men were real all-action heroes and the spectacle had the same sense of drama that had inspired me when I watched spacemen landing on the moon a few years earlier. It was the power of pure entertainment and this time I noticed something extra. I was looking at the women as they watched and they were definitely impressed. This is the job for me, I thought.

By this time I'd moved up to Dudley Middle School. I was a small fish in a bigger pond and for the first time I was thrown in with kids from other villages, not just the local lads. Most of my friends were girls, and that never changed, but at this stage I also began to see girls in a different light. The problem was trying to get them to see me the same way. Maybe parachuting would work where acting had so far failed, I decided.

When we got back to school I duly tried it out on Karen Aitken, the current apple of my eye. Determined to impress her, I spent weeks leaping off walls, garage roofs and fences with my shirt billowing behind me. Without the aid of a parachute, it hurt, of course, but I had her attention and that was what mattered.

My career as a Red Devil culminated with a planned double leap from our bedroom window. I'd managed to rope our David in with a convincing argument that we could fly. Enthusiastic powers of persuasion were my forte; I had recently convinced David's mate Michael Stanley that I could go to the moon in the shed — a story he continued to believe for years.

Mam was at work, Dad was asleep and Dawn was in charge. The bedroom windows opened right out, so we were standing on a precipice. As we stood on the edge, complete with red pyjamas and bed sheets as makeshift capes, it momentarily crossed my mind that this was a really stupid idea. But it was too late to back down. We'd attracted an audience of neighbours by now, shouting, 'Look, it's the Greens' laddies hanging out the window.' Presumably the commotion woke my dad, because just short of our intended moment of glory we were dragged in through the window and given a belting. 'There's a lot more where that came from' we heard for the zillionth time. That was the end of the Red Devils phase.

If Devon that year was a winner, the least successful family holiday was camping in Scotland the year after. The plan was to head north, pitch our tent and enjoy the countryside for two weeks. We lasted twenty-four hours.

It was doomed from the start. My dad was always a man in a hurry and in the rush to get away, my mam, preoccupied with getting four overexcited kids out of the house, left half the

stuff behind. By the time she realized, we were well past the border. We arrived to sheets of lashing rain and after a desperate struggle with tent pegs and groundsheets we tried to settle down – packed in like refugees, cold and damp and so uncomfortable we couldn't sleep. My dad rarely spent more than a few hours a week in our company and now we were all going to spend two weeks sleeping together in the same tent. It was a ludicrous idea and obvious that he wasn't going to be able to stand it for more than a few hours. David and I were crying, Joanna was trying to keep us quiet and Mam was trying to keep Dad quiet. Halfway through the night we were ordered to pack our stuff, and then we drove home. I've never been camping since.

There wasn't much talking with my dad as kids. Male emotions are suppressed in that kind of environment and it wasn't until much later that we started to talk. He was a large presence but while he had authority and received respect, it was my mum I went to when I needed to talk. She was sensitive and compassionate. We were, and still are, very close. For Mam, smacking was a last resort, and she only ever whacked me once. It was Christmas and, not really realizing it was something my parents couldn't afford, I was desperate for an elaborate Scalextric set. It was the one that went round the whole living room, had bridges, intersections, overtaking lanes, the lot, and I had been talking about it for weeks. Come Christmas morning, the set I unwrapped didn't live up to expectations. It was a single circular track about two feet in diameter. I cried that it wasn't the one I wanted, eventually jumping up and down on the cars in temper and smashing them. I deserved all I got. I was scared of her for a little while after, but it didn't last long.

Although he himself was a firm believer in smacking, Dad would go ballistic if I was in fights

DUDLEY MIDDLE SCHOOL CROSS-COUNTRY TEAM. TOP, FROM LEFT: PAUL GRANGER, PAUL CHERRY, NIGEL HORGAN. FRONT: ME AND DAVID STANLEY.

as a kid. In fact he had little to worry about. He had taught us to look after ourselves, but I was never a fighter by choice. On one occasion I was given a hard time by Keith Hudson – ours was always a bit of a love-hate relationship – and came home with my nose bleeding. Dad wasn't a violent man, but he wasn't going to raise his sons to be softies either. He stood up for himself and he wanted us to be able to as well. He gave me a stick and my orders: 'Take that stick and gi' 'im what for.' 'Please, Dad, I don't want to,' I sobbed, but he insisted. Fighting back tears, I advanced on Keith with my stick. He promptly grabbed it and beat the shit out of me instead. It might have worked for my dad, but it didn't for me, and just confirmed that when faced with trouble my best bet was to talk my way out of it ... or run.

Keith and I soon patched it up – at least enough to appear as a double act at the Miners' Gala soon after. The galas, or 'welfares' as they were known, took place twice a year all over the north-east and had replaced chapel as the chance to perform to a crowd. The local miners would chip in a few pence in the pound from their wages to fund them. There were stalls, a fun fair and talent competitions, and as you went in you were given two pounds to spend on whatever you wanted.

The highlight for me was the talent competition, which I won on my second attempt, singing Charlie Rich's country and western classic *The Most Beautiful Girl In The World.* There was no band, no backing track – just this tiny ten-year-old belting out, 'I woke up this morning, realized what I had done...' Again my sisters had been there before me. Both had been singing in the galas since they were old enough to learn a set of lyrics, and some years Dawn, Joanna and I would all be in competition against each other. Joanna won one year, singing *Ave Maria* with Helen Jeffries, and even went on to audition for the TV show *Opportunity Knocks*.

At another gala, me, Alan Wardle, Paul Story and Keith Hudson – who would only join the band because you stood to win £15 – did *Blockbuster*, the old Sweet number. We couldn't play any instruments and mimed, but to compensate we dressed up in all the Indian gear plus full make-up. Sweet were pretty camp and I was the guy who shrieked in rock-style falsetto, 'Haven't got a clooo what to do.' When we didn't get through to the finals I was mortified and still had to face my dad afterwards to explain the glitter eye-shadow and blusher.

The next year things got even worse. I was eleven and Keith and I decided to do a duet: Laurel and Hardy's *Blue Ridge Mountains Of Virginia.* Keith couldn't sing, but he excelled at the part where he had to hit me on the head with a mallet. This time we came second, beaten by Darkie Purvis doing a spectacular Gary Glitter number.

I learned my lesson. The next year I went solo, with *Love Is In The Air*. I won, but had my thunder stolen by Barrie Maddison, who entered himself as a comedy act. It wasn't going too well to start with: his jokes were going down like farts in a spacesuit until suddenly, inspired to overstep the mark and go for a grand finale, he came out with, 'What's the difference between a JCB and a giraffe…? One's got hydraulics and the other's got high bollocks.' The crowd went wild as he was dragged off the stage by his dad for a hiding.

At eleven I started the daily twenty-minute walk to Seaton Burn High, which was an even tougher school. Gang frictions were a regular occurrence and as a small, wimpy-looking kid I was a target for bullies. As usual, I threw myself into music and acting, joining the school orchestra and whatever else was going. Again Dawn had already set a precedent. She and three friends had formed a group called the Soda Pops who toured old people's homes singing folk music and country and western, and even appeared on telly once in a northern music festival. But the girls stuck with singing. Acting was left open for me to make my mark.

The main after-school pursuit was girls. From about age twelve we had a point system, starting with one point for a kiss and peaking at five. There was lots of talk of sexual adventures, but you could only ever believe half of it. The whole thing was quite hard for me because I was never much of a hit. The boys getting all the real action were the hard lads in the village. My high point was a two.

AT SEATON BURN HIGH SCHOOL. I'M IN THE MIDDLE ROW, SECOND FROM LEFT, WITH STEVEN 'THE PROFESSOR' WILLIAMSON ON THE FAR RIGHT.

WITH MY NEPHEW DAYMON OUTSIDE OUR HOUSE IN WANSBECK ROAD.

Jane Lyall was the object of my desire and rather than wait for her to notice me I thought I'd get the ball rolling and write my own graffiti on the school lockers: 'Jane Lyall fancies Robson Green.' It failed dismally. Instead I went out with Agnes Barrass, the javelin thrower. I had a bit of a wait before Shirley Waugh eventually supplied me with my first proper kiss and eventually started going out with Dawn Taylor. 'Going out' with girls usually meant meeting up after school and hanging about. No one had the money to do much else.

The main thing was the sense of freedom we got from being out of the home and away from the watchful eye of the grown-ups. A favourite haunt was the burn and the giant disused sewer pipes we found there. They made great dens and when it was windy and bitter we would block off one end and get inside. They were little worlds for us when we were small and later became a handy place to take a girlfriend. Nowadays you could huddle in McDonald's; then it was a date at the sewage pipes. Cosy, if not exactly romantic.

By the time I was twelve my parents had decided to divorce. It was unusual then and not talked about much, but they weren't happy together; I could tell. A year later they were living separately. It was a brave thing to do, but at the time I wanted to hide it and only really talked about it with David, at night in our room.

With Mam and Dad separated and Dawn too old for family holidays, Mam decided to take me and David to Spain that year. It was the first time Mam had flown and the first time any of us had been abroad. It was late September 1980 and we were going to Minorca. Joanna was working, so she paid for herself and took two friends from work.

Travelling abroad for the first time, I had high hopes; a foreign country, another language, exotic seafood and, of course, beautiful Spanish girls. But somehow, from the minute we boarded the plane to a chorus of *Viva España*, I knew it was not going to live up to expectations. The resort was Little England with sunshine. Everywhere I looked tourists sat roasting in the midday heat, ploughing through traditional English breakfasts, washed down with imported English beers. I had as about as much chance of meeting a Spaniard as I did in Newcastle.

My mam did her best to show us something more interesting, but without a car or much cash she was fighting a losing battle. To make things worse, things got off to a sticky start when Joanna went straight into the windscreen of a car after a night of clubbing with her mates. After a detour to the local hospital for fourteen stitches she arrived back at the villa to break the news and, despite taking the precaution of sending her friends ahead to warn my mam, it was a dramatic sight. She had been wearing a white, Crimplene halter-neck dress and the material had soaked up the blood like a tissue. She looked like an extra from *Nightmare on Elm Street*. My mam took one look at her and threw up over the balcony.

It was a fortnight's holiday and by the second week we'd run out of money after overspending wildly in the first few days. I remember being in a restaurant and knowing Mam didn't have enough to pay for a meal for all of us. She was working out the cheapest meal and going without herself. Now we were well and truly stuck. I had wanted to come back with stories about this exotic place that we'd visited, people that we'd met, remote hilltop villages, Flamenco dancing. Instead we were stranded in an overdeveloped resort full of English tourists.

By now Dawn was on the verge of leaving home too. She must have been keen to get out to work after spending her early teens watching out for us lot. As soon as she got home from school she'd have to start on the tea and take care of the housework. We'd be driving her up the wall, bickering and getting under her feet and she would be half demented trying to get everything right. As a kid I couldn't understand why she had such a thing about tidiness. I guess it was because she was the one who was in for it if the place was a mess. But she got her own back.

To my mam's horror, Dawn had started smoking as a teenager and had to find a way to subsidize her habit. That was when she hit on the idea of charging us for making our breakfast at weekends when my parents were having a lie-in. To be fair, she would set it up like a buffet, with 'gypsy toast', dipped in egg, fried and cut up into neat squares, and red and brown sauce for dipping. It was two pence for plain gypsy toast, three pence for toast with brown sauce and five pence for red because she knew it was our favourite. Sunday mornings were the worst. My mam would get up at seven to put the joint in the oven and by eleven o'clock the smell of the slowly roasting beef was mouth-watering. At ten pence a shot, Dawn would dip fingers of bread into the juices and serve them up as a treat. David and I never had any money, so Joanna would have to pay for us out of her babysitting money. If we didn't pay we didn't get it.

Something else she did only came out a few years ago, and Joanna wouldn't speak to her for a week after she found out. At Christmas Mam would put our names up over the mantelpiece in the sitting room and stack up our presents with a pile under each name. After listening for Mam and Dad to go up to bed, Dawn would give them an hour to drop off and then get up and come downstairs. She'd look to see what everybody had and swap them around, taking what she wanted for herself. If Joanna's slippers were pink and Dawn's were blue she'd swap them over. If David and I had better sweets they would end up in Dawn's pile. We never knew. It was her guilty secret for thirty-odd years.

Dawn didn't bother to sit her leaving exams. When she heard there was a telephonist's job going nearby, she took it. She was fifteen and at an age when she wanted things for herself as well as wanting to help out at home. Within a few months my dad's youngest brother, Uncle Matheson, opened up a hairdressing business and she went to work for him. As an apprentice she came out with only £15 a week, but she claims she partly took the job to save us from any more of my mam's terrible haircuts. Until Dawn took over, David looked like Shirley Temple on a bad day and I looked like my hair had been cut with a knife and fork.

A few years later Dawn needed a model and I was the only one who would let her have a go. She was on a colouring course and I ended up the only thirteen-year-old in Newcastle with two-tone crimson hair. Around that time I went to Blackpool with my dad. The illuminations were meant to be the attraction, but I was definitely in it for the girls and with my knockout new hair I reckoned I couldn't fail. We hit the town on the first night and I spotted her right away: small, dark and timid. I stood for a while, feeling confident,

WITH PHILLIP BELL, A GUITARIST WITH SOLID STATE, ON THE NIGHT OF MY EIGHTEENTH BIRTHDAY AT THE DUDLEY AND WEETSLADE SOCIAL CLUB.

with my tipped hair, white T-shirt, flares and plat-forms, staring gormlessly at this girl across the dance floor. Assuming she was just waiting for the nod, I swaggered over, glass in hand, thinking wedded bliss was just around the corner.

'Where you from?'

'Wales.'

'Dance?'

'No.'

'All right.'

Dawn married at eighteen. It was a whirlwind romance; she and Derek met in September, got engaged the following January and she was expecting by March. There was only one hitch. In the time-honoured tradition, the wedding wasn't scheduled until the following September. The doctor who delivered the good news was a father of six. His words to her were simply: 'Remember, this is your first baby.' In other words there was never any question of whether or not she would have the baby (although in Dawn and Derek's case he was to be the first and last: with Derek one of six and Dawn one of four, they decided they wanted a quieter life). The baby wasn't really the problem. The problem was telling my dad. Uncle Matheson, whom she told at work the day she found out, advised her to tell the truth right away as she was going to have to sooner or later.

When we all sat down to dinner that night, something was obviously up. She had considered bringing Derek back – they were engaged after all – but then realized Dad would probably kill him. Instead she had come straight home from work, tidied up and set the table before Mam and Dad got back. She was noticeably nervous, but waited until we had finished eating before getting things off her chest.

'Dad, I've got something to tell you'.

'What?'

'Dad … I'm, well, I'm … pregnant.'

Caught between rage and shock, Dad struggled for a response, 'Well, that's it!' he thundered. 'The big wedding's off.'

Dawn had planned a big do, and in temper this was Dad's only way of punishing her. It was a big thing, the marriage of his first daughter, and he and Mam had been working overtime to pay for it.

They got over it, of course, and the wedding was duly brought forward.

For me and the Hudson lads, weddings meant one thing: a 'hoy out', one of the most popular traditions in the north-east at the time, particularly with kids. According to tradition, the family collect all their small change together and the bride and her father throw it from the car as they pull away from the church. If you knew there was a wedding on within a five-mile radius you were off to see what you could pick up. Not content to leave things to chance, the Hudsons and I had formulated a plan for Dawn's big day. I was to sit in the back of the wedding car next to the window. When the time came to chuck out the change, Keith and Colin were positioned just outside the window. Every penny went straight into their jumpers, held out conveniently like collecting bowls.

So it was a great day for Dawn and Derek after all, and a lucrative one for me and the Hudson lads, but it was left to Dad to provide the surreal and dramatic climax. Wedding or not, no one was prepared for the sight of a bladdered Robson senior riding up the high street like one

VISITING AN RAF GRAVE-YARD WHILE IN HOLLAND WITH THE ATC.

28

of the Magnificent Seven, astride a horse he had borrowed for the occasion. To this day I don't know what possessed him, but somehow it provided a fitting end to a memorable day.

And so Dawn was gone too. Derek was a miner at Seaton Burn pit and once married the two of them lived with Derek's mam, a widower, who lived just up the road. They were there for a year saving for the flat and it was a hard slog. Dawn has never been out of work and was out doing someone's hair the night before her son Daymon was born.

In theory we had a lot more freedom once Dad and Dawn had both moved out. In reality nothing much changed. I missed the security Dad's presence had provided and although I was allowed to stay out a bit later and was part of a local gang as everyone was, I managed to keep out of trouble.

We would meet down at the burn which ran through Dudley and look for something to occupy ourselves. This was usually fairly innocent stuff like Knocky Nine Doors and at its worst stretched to pinching David Clarke's chopper bike. As usual, I was the lookout because I was too much of a coward to actually do the deed. The next thing I knew the cops were at the door – under pressure the other kids had snitched on me – and I knew there was no acting my way out of this one. The fear was all-consuming and facing my dad once the police had left was enough to keep me out of trouble from then on.

Television still dominated my time indoors. I'd watch anything but was a sucker for high drama and easily the most emotional of the four of us. Caught crying by Joanna at the tragic finale of *The King and I* – as the hand drops and you know he's died – I tried to hide my tears, claiming I had something in my eye. When this happened during *West Side Story* and again during the nth rerun of

It's a Wonderful Life, I gave up making excuses.

The bane of my life was the meter. We were a house on tick and anything that could be run on meters was, including the telly. Life was governed by a constant search for fifty-pence pieces. We'd be watching a great film on TV and suddenly the screen would go blank and there would be a mad scramble to feed the meter. No fifties, no TV. If we were desperate we'd run up to Mrs Wardle, who kept a stock of fifties because she knew the Greens would be round. On the rare occasion that I brought a girlfriend back there would always be the risk that halfway through the evening we'd all be plunged into total darkness. It wasn't great for my image.

We were always on the lookout for French and Italian films, because breasts were pretty much guaranteed. Movies showed you women as you never saw them in life, even if the most interesting parts were covered.

ON AN ATC TRIP TO CYPRUS.

If Mam and Dad were around, though, we could forget it; any hint of sex on screen, even heavy kissing scenes, and an early bedtime was on the cards. Although I was sexually aware from a young age and extremely curious, sex certainly wasn't discussed at home. Sex education at school was basic and biological and by the time that came along I'd figured things out for myself anyway.

There's no doubt that part of the appeal of acting at school was the pulling power I hoped would come with it. I'd seen it done on the telly, after all. Women and girls would swoon at the mere sight of Paul Newman, Bogie and Montgomery Clift. Surely a bit of make-up, a costume and a few moving speeches would guarantee a lass, I thought, but somehow it never quite worked out that way. Even though my appearance in *Dracula Spectacular* made the desired impression, it still backfired in the end. Sure enough, Tracy Liddell decided I was the one for her after my impressive performance as a zombie, but what I hadn't reckoned on were the repercussions. Tracy was the school sweetheart and particularly popular with all the hardest guys in the year. When she wrote on her school file 'Tracy loves Robson' she might as well have put my name on a hit list. It went round the school like wildfire and I had to spend a few weeks in hiding. There was only one thing for it – start a rock band.

Solid State got going when I was fifteen. It was yet another stab at showbiz and there was always an outside chance that it might attract some girls. Mam had bought me an electric guitar at twelve or thirteen, a red and yellow model with a sun-burst finish, plus a five-watt amp. I'd been wearing my fingers out trying to learn *House Of The Rising Sun* ever since and was itching to move on to bigger things.

We rehearsed in St Paul's Church, Dudley, where the vicar let us use a side room. It was me, Steven Williamson, Robert, John 'Curly' Davis (on account of his Afro), Phillip Bell and Kevin Hughes on drums. Kevin was the brother of the gorgeous Helen Hughes, so he was in like a shot as soon as he showed a glimmer of interest; any drumming ability was a bonus. Rehearsal breaks revolved around me looking for an opportunity to sidle over with, 'Umm … by the way, how's Helen?' I was desperate to hear she might have mentioned me, but in fact she hadn't even noticed me. Unfortunately my confidence on stage didn't extend to girls and I was far too smitten to actually speak to Helen in person. My only point of contact would be the Christmas school disco and if I failed to get a dance I had to wait a whole year for another opportunity.

I was the lead singer and we performed at school dances, in the lunch hour, in assembly and wherever else they'd have us. My stage gear featured a pair of trousers with a huge S running down one leg and 'OLID TATE' emblazoned across the other. I'd introduce us by shouting 'Ladies and gentlemen, we are…' and on cue I'd throw my knees together. It was our idea of spe-

CAMPING IN THE LAKE DISTRICT. LEFT TO RIGHT: JOE CAFFREY, DEAN MARRINER (BOTH OF THE WORKY TICKETS) AND ME.

cial effects and we thought it was brilliant, or at least I did. We drank milk on stage and mimicked what we thought were classic rock moves. We did a few covers, like Gary Numan's *Cars*, but mostly wrote our own material; it fell into two categories – relationships and teen angst. We would open with a song called *Three Minute Warning* about the threat of nuclear attack:

Screechin' cross the sky, wah, wah, wah.
Don't know why, wah, wah, wah.
We only got three minutes.
It's a warning.

Dire stuff but we thought it was pretty cool. *Utopia* ran along the same lines:

Cities of the Future,
People with one mind.
They have lost emotions,
Left them all behind.

Nothing is perfect,
Nothing remains the same,
Everybody's going to die
But that's the game
Utopia, Utopia, Utopia, Utopia.

To catch us live in the lunch-hour cost five pence, but Colin Hudson always got in for free and in return I got his valuable services as a critic. When I'd put my knees together to form 'SOLID STATE' he'd shake his head in disbelief. We even had a couple of groupies to complete the image: two girls, one of whom wore the most fantastic spray-on trousers which at fifteen really did wonders for me.

We thought we'd really cracked it when we were invited to play for the mayor on his visit to the school. We decided to play *Child In Time*, the Deep Purple song which, on the original, features Ian Gillan doing an impressive screaming solo in the middle. We were so nervous that the screeching went a bit awry and the mayor, looking appalled, left halfway through while the band played on. Somehow nothing fazed me. Anyone else would have been deeply embarrassed by the whole thing, from the low-tech knees-together special

effects to the on-stage posturing, and the other guys in the band probably were. They were actually the real musicians, but I had the front.

At fifteen I had my most serious crush. Donna Potts was The One and I knew it was love even if she didn't know what my name was. I never stopped thinking about her and couldn't concentrate on anything else. Unfortunately, if she so much as glanced in my general direction when we passed in the corridor I completely overreacted, babbling like an idiot. Testosterone was in top gear by now and, inspired by *Grease* (which I'd seen six times), I went through a John Travolta phase – greased hair and a black fake-leather jacket on which I'd Tippexed the words 'T Birds'. As far as I was concerned, if it worked for John it could work for me.

My confidence was bolstered by my mate Paul Story, who assured me Donna was secretly interested. It was a wind-up I should have seen a mile off, but I was blinded by love. Eventually, after assembly one day, I made my move. While Donna had been uppermost in my mind for at least a year, I was a complete stranger to her, a weedy little guy in a Tippexed jacket. Undaunted, I didn't beat about the bush: 'Donna, will you go out with us?'. The response was crushing. The look said 'Who the hell are you?' while her mouth seemed to be saying 'No'. It was hard to hear over the eruption of giggling from her mates. I was getting used to rejection.

Somewhere along the line I developed military aspirations and moved into my 'anorak' stage. We lived on a major flight path so I could stand outside with my binoculars, reference book and pad, spotting planes. It's sad but true that to this day I can still recognize a Fokker, a Buccaneer, an F15 or a Russian Bear.

The appeal was basic and uncomplicated – I liked planes that went fast and made a lot of noise. Beyond that I didn't think it through – just threw myself into it one hundred per cent, as I did with everything else. I even joined the Air Training Corps at sixteen and travelled to Cyprus with them to practise mock RAF drills and learn about the principles of flight.

In direct contrast, at around the same age I also got involved with the Labour Party, canvassing,

A REHEARSAL BREAK
DURING *THE LONG LINE*
AT THE LIVE THEATRE,
NEWCASTLE, IN 1986.
FROM LEFT: ME, GAVIN
KITCHEN, BRIAN HOGG,
FELICITY FINCH, CHRISSY
EDGE, PAULINE MORIARTY
AND THE PLAYWRIGHT,
TOM HADAWAY.

discipline came easy to them, as did the assumption that they were officer material, but I was worlds away socially and financially. When I looked around me and wondered whether I could survive alongside these guys I knew the answer was no. More importantly, it had *finally* dawned on me that the sole purpose of these planes I was so fascinated by was to kill people.

I was very interested in the war years. At sixteen I'd read William Shirer's *The Rise and Fall of the Third Reich* because I wanted to know where fascism came from, particularly because the Nazi party had begun as a working-class movement. TV programmes like *The World at War* fascinated me for the same reasons. It took a while to realize that my interest in war was about the why rather than the how.

Even as a teenager with the ATC I should have realized I was on completely the wrong path. On one occasion we went somewhere in the south of England for a weekend of exercises and one night had to simulate an attack on an enemy base. The guys running the exercise were non-commissioned officers, working-class guys who would never make it beyond a certain rank because they hadn't been to the right school. They were hard men and this was a rare opportunity to be in charge even if we were only a gang of kids.

At first it was exciting. We were kitted out in camouflage gear and our faces smeared with mud, then sent out into the woods. Next thing we knew we were captured, someone pulled sacks over our heads and started punching us in the belly and firing questions at us. All this was supposed to lend a realistic feel to a kids' exercise. In retrospect it was a crowd of grown men acting out an aggressive power fantasy. Whatever it was, it wasn't for me.

That left acting and the shipyard.

sticking up posters and helping people get to the polling station. I was motivated by what I could see around me and as idealistic as most sixteen-year-olds, so that by the end of the year I was slightly to the left of Arthur Scargill.

With only a year or so left at school I started to think about a career. I was both very focused and unsure. I knew without a shadow of a doubt that I wanted to act, but I also knew I needed to earn a living and the two didn't marry up. I had a good engineering mind and there was talk of an apprenticeship at Swan Hunter, the local shipbuilder. There was also the possibility of a military career, although a week's introductory course at Biggin Hill soon ruled that out.

Right away I had a problem with the discipline, and the class set-up was also a major barrier. Everybody else on the course came from public school or boarding school and their fathers and grandfathers had had careers in the RAF. Military

I t was my last year at Seaton Burn High School. The exams were all that separated me from a school life free of responsibility and the new world of work. Always in a hurry, I sat two A levels in a year: Engineering Drawing and Design Technology. These subjects had provided the opportunity at Biggin Hill and now also gave me the chance to train as an apprentice draughtsman at the shipyard. The apprenticeship was a big step up as far as my parents were concerned. It was a steady job with prospects and although it wasn't exactly what I had in mind, I was by this time seventeen and keen to start earning.I had briefly contemplated university and drama school but neither seemed feasible. I didn't want to move away and I hadn't got the exam

THE YEAR OF LIVING DANGEROUSLY

results, having failed maths and physics at O level. To everyone's surprise but my own I had also failed O-level drama. For the exam I played Orsino in *Twelfth Night*, but didn't have a clue what I was talking about. To make things worse, I was encouraged to change my delivery, trading in Geordie for Received Pronunciation. The way I approached acting, even at that age, was to develop the part as an extension of my personality and in Shakespeare I found nothing I could relate to. The same applied to literature. The only book that had any kind of impact on me was George Orwell's *Animal Farm*. The rest completely passed me by.

Although there were always a few good teachers who tried their best with the curriculum they were given, I received encouragement not so much through school but from Max Roberts. More than anyone else, he is the reason I'm doing what I am today.

I had first met Max when he came backstage after the school production of *Dracula Spectacular*. He explained that he ran a youth theatre in Backworth and wanted to involve some local kids. Although he had singled me out and asked if I'd drop by I didn't take him up on it at the time. It was only in my last year, when the school arranged for us to do a stage-fighting course at Backworth, that we recognized each other and I remembered his offer. We got chatting and he asked if I would like to come to Backworth on a regular basis after school or work. I decided to give it a go.

At around the same time the offer of a four-year draughtsman's apprenticeship at Swan Hunter came through. I signed on the dotted line: £155 on the table each week was not something I could afford to turn down. I was still at home and the contribution was a relief for my mam. Besides, it was a privilege to get an apprenticeship at a time when unemployment was so widespread. My parents were proud and my teacher, Harry Robson, was delighted that something he'd taught me had got me started.

The job was seen as the first rung on the ladder to a steady career. No one could know the shipyards would be closed within the decade. Although I knew within a matter of weeks that it wasn't the career I wanted or would end up in, I was determined to stick it out. I put in the hours and did the job well, but for me the day started when I clocked off and set off for Backworth on my bike.

The most striking thing about the Backworth Youth Theatre was the material Max presented us with. The plays were a revelation: local stories by local writers. Unlike school, there was no effort involved in relating to the characters or the language because the plays were rooted in our own regional culture and written in words and phrases we used every day.

When I joined they were putting together a play called *Francie Nichol* and Max had me in mind for the male lead. Based on a true story about a famous boxer from North Shields called Johnny Robinson, the book had been written by Joe Robinson and adapted for us by local playwright Tom Hadaway. The play centred on the doomed love affair between Johnny and a young woman named Francie Nichol. Francie is an outsider, from a different area, and Johnny's family's refusal to accept her leads the couple to become isolated. While he fights his way towards the championship, she is reduced to cleaning lodgings, and caring for their new baby, until one night, thinking Johnny is due to return, she leaves the baby alone and it is killed in a fire.

It was a great part in a brilliant play. I couldn't have asked for more. Max was so pleased with the production, it was decided we would take it to Edinburgh for the festival that summer.

Edinburgh was a fantastic eye-opener. There was theatre everywhere, on every street corner and in every available venue. Theatre groups had come from all over the country and the plays were incredibly diverse, from Robert Tressell's *The Ragged Trousered Philanthropists*, by the Metro Theatre Company, to The National Theatre of Brent doing a two-man comedy version of *The Messiah*. Suddenly a new world opened up to me. I'd seen great theatre in Newcastle, but to find regional theatre groups doing such a range of material was really an education.

It was in Edinburgh that I got to know Joe Caffrey. Our paths had crossed earlier when my school visited his, not far away, to see their production of *Oklahoma*, but we only met later when

both of us were recruited by Max to join Backworth. He made me laugh from the first time we met. Like all good comics, Joe is a natural. He rarely told jokes, but had a knack for turning the smallest incident into something hilarious, and just being with him was a guarantee of a good time.

Backworth opened up other opportunities for travel, but it wasn't always easy getting time off from the shipyard. Between seventeen and twenty-one I found myself saving up my holidays to act just as my dad had done at the same age in order to dance.

In 1982 we went to Berlin. The trip was run as a drama student exchange funded by the Labour government, and staying with a German family made it a cultural experience as well as a chance to act. We were touring with a play by Peter Mortimer called *Imagine*, which predicted the end of the world because people couldn't live together in peace. Nice idea, but the script needed saving. Max suggested introducing songs and the result was an a cappella musical.

There were a lot of strong singers at Backworth and that was where we sang together for the first time. Not only did it rescue the play, but it was fun. On our return to Newcastle we decided to make something of it.

We started small. Practice often took place at my house and the eight of us started to get a repertoire together. Our inspiration was the Flying Pickets, a politically like-minded a cappella group who had recently had a hit with *Only You*. In homage, I suppose, we became the Worky Tickets. Initially we busked, mostly outside Woolworths in the city centre and occasionally worked the Metro system, jumping on the trains and breaking into a cappella versions of Phil Spector numbers like the Crystals' *Then He Kissed Me* and *Da Doo Ron Ron* by the Ronettes.

Joanna always looked in when we rehearsed at home, but David did what he could to make himself scarce. Chalk and cheese is what they say. David, tall, shy and quiet, was as different from me as he could be. He'd come home from working at the farm and we'd be there, seven or eight of us, singing and playing guitars. He'd always head

PERFORMING WITH THE WORKY TICKETS AT THE CONSETT EMPIRE DURING THE MINERS' STRIKE OF 1984. LEFT TO RIGHT: DEAN MARRINER, ME, GILL BURRIDGE, PAULA HOLLAND, SHELLEY AND ALI BURRIDGE (WHO LATER MARRIED JOE CAFFREY).

straight upstairs to the bedroom and let us get on with it. Even later, when the family would come to cast parties, he was always less comfortable with the acting crowd than the others. We must have seemed like a terrible crowd of exhibitionists to him. He was never excluded, but it just wasn't his thing.

Things were going well. After busking for about a year we got asked to do local gigs, then ended up doing a few TV spots, singing *The Wanderer* on a regional TV programme called *The Works*, presented by Muriel Gray, and appearing on *Swap Shop* in 1983. When my sisters came to see us supporting a big club band in North Shields it was the first time they'd really seen me on a stage, standing in my overalls, like a working-class uniform, and Joanna loved it. Even David was impressed when he saw me on the telly.

Work at Backworth was going equally well and my love life even better. Shelley was my first real love. We went back a long way. Like me, she used to sing at the miners' galas and was so mortified when I beat her into second place one year that she locked herself in the toilets afterwards and refused to come out. As teenagers we were at Seaton Burn High together, but she was two years younger than me and at that age it seemed like a decade.

I had first set my heart on her at seventeen. On the strength of my singing with Solid State, Mr Beckett, the music teacher had offered me the part of Frederick in the school production of *The Pirates of Penzance*. Frederick had two missions in life, to escape the clutches of the pirate king and to get into Mabel's knickers. Shelley was cast as Mabel. What a voice, and those eyes. She looked the loveliest creature and throughout rehearsals I couldn't stop thinking about her.

My opportunity finally came a year later when Mam was away for a weekend and I decide to take advantage and throw a party. All I had to do was invite her.

'Shelley … erm … I'm having a party. Could you, I mean, would you … what I mean is, will you come?'

As soon as the words were out, I was panicking. She was fifteen. A schoolgirl of fifteen to my on-the-verge-of-adulthood seventeen. People would think I was a pervert. *She* would think I was a pervert.

'When and what time will it finish?' she replied at last.

'So that's a yes then?'

'Yes.'

Yes, yes, yes. She said yes. So what if other people thought I was a cradle snatcher? – she said yes. It was the beginning of a seven-year relationship. A relationship based on love, passion, friendship, parties and, above all, great fun. By the time we were singing together with the Worky Tickets it qualified as a serious relationship, or at least as serious as it could be given that I was in overdrive at the time and both of us were trying to carve out our own careers.

The next big Backworth production was *Bandits*, another adaptation of a true story from the northeast, this time written by a hero of Max's, C.P. Taylor. Set in 1967, it told the story of Michael LaVaglio and Dennis Stafford, wrongly imprisoned for fifteen years for the murder of a small-time crook called Angus Sibbet. The title refers to the one-arm bandits which at the time provided a healthy income for the big boys of organized crime. Sibbet was fiddling the bandits, but when he started flashing the cash around too conspicuously someone was sent up from London to bump him off and his body was found by a Tyneside miner. The murderers walked free, while two local men were accused and convicted of the murder.

It was a fantastic story. I played Inspector Bridges, a great comic part with a lot of direct-to-audience dialogue. Instead of having his mind on the case, the inspector is completely absorbed in his own problems: his caravan in the country and a feud with a neighbour. It did so well that we took it to the Shaw Theatre in London. The reviews were great and people still say that our youth theatre production was better than any other they have seen since, including a version by the RSC. Among our admirers was Simon Curtis, who many years later would direct me in his first production for television, *The Prince of Hearts*.

Nineteen eighty-four was the year of the miners' strike. The predictions of Arthur Scargill, President of the National Miners' Union, were coming true. All over the north of England pits were closing,

men were losing their jobs and families were struggling to make ends meet. I could see the effects on my doorstep. With Dawn's husband Derek on strike, they were barely managing on her hairdressing wages and my mam and neighbours often helped out with food parcels. Wanting to show solidarity, the Worky Tickets started touring clubs to raise money. Our finest hour came when we were asked to play alongside Billy Bragg, the Flying Pickets and Paul Weller at the Royal Albert Hall. The show was a fund-raising show and we were proud to be part of it.

Meeting Scargill after another fund-raiser in Sheffield was a huge privilege. I saw him as a man who never compromised. When he warned of the decimation of the pit communities, the destruction of the NUM and with it the end of the organized working class, he was ridiculed as a paranoid extremist. Now it's history – the whole sequence of events had been plotted by Thatcher and Peter Walker, the Secretary of State for Energy. It was brilliantly executed and it worked. The human consequences

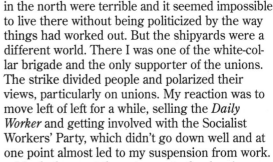

PERFORMING IN SHEFFIELD, WHERE I WAS PROUD TO MEET MINERS' UNION LEADER ARTHUR SCARGILL.

in the north were terrible and it seemed impossible to live there without being politicized by the way things had worked out. But the shipyards were a different world. There I was one of the white-collar brigade and the only supporter of the unions. The strike divided people and polarized their views, particularly on unions. My reaction was to move left of left for a while, selling the *Daily Worker* and getting involved with the Socialist Workers' Party, which didn't go down well and at one point almost led to my suspension from work.

My desk was at the entrance to the drawing office and the 'Coal Not Dole' poster I stuck on the wall there was repeatedly torn down. Although the strike was originally about miners' working conditions, health and safety, it turned into a head-on confrontation with Thatcherism. The response at work was, 'What're they complaining about? I bet they earn more than me.' To me, the comparison was ludicrous. Men doing a desk job – as I was then – had no idea what real work was and as far as I was concerned the miners deserved every penny.

It was an odd situation. The work at the shipyards was OK and aspects of it, for example working on the design for ships like the *Ark Royal* and the *Coventry*, were something to be proud of. At the same time I had no more in common with the guys there than I now had with the lads I had been at school with. I was out of step with the crowd and radically different in my attitude towards politics, women, race – in fact, pretty much everything. When they were down the pub, I was on my way to rehearsal. Even if I was in the pub, I wasn't one of the lads. I didn't tell or laugh at racist or sexist jokes and I was appalled by things like strippergrams, which were popular at the time. When I first arrived at the shipyard and found the walls plastered with dirty calendars, I asked for them to be taken down. So I was singled out very early on.

Having gone from strength to strength, Max Roberts was offered a job running Newcastle's Live Theatre,

which meant a move from amateur to professional. Without an Equity card, I was temporarily out of the picture. While I was at Backworth I had always had my regular income from Swan Hunter, but now I was in the final stages of my apprenticeship. I would soon have to decide between staying at the shipyard and leaving to become a professional actor.

When I was in my last year at Swan Hunter, Max opened with a play called *Hanging About* which coincided with the end of the miners' strike. It was about what it had done to the lives of two miners, and was written by Pauline Hadaway, the daughter of Tom.

It was a boom time for small theatre groups which were playing to workers in pubs and clubs right across the north. At the same time there was a disturbing move towards tampering with scripts in order to make them more overtly political. Rather than moving people to the left as intended, this alienated them from the plays by placing the emphasis too heavily on political comment at the expense of entertainment. The beauty of Max's productions was that the politics were implicit in the writing. They didn't hit you over the head with a message and send you running for

BANDITS, 1988, AT THE LIVE THEATRE WITH PHILLIPA WILSON, WHO LATER PLAYED MY GIRLFRIEND IN *THE PRINCE OF HEARTS*.

39

the door. The focus was on individuals and their lives and relationships.

Without an Equity card I wasn't in the running for *Hanging About,* although I was still socializing with Max and some of the actors at the Live Theatre. It was difficult to be on the sidelines as Max moved on to bigger and better things, but fortunately he had plans for me. One evening he asked me to pop into the Corner House, a pub in Heaton. Max and I were alone playing pool and I was biding my time waiting to see what it was he wanted to talk about.

'We're doing a play called *The Long Line,*' he began. 'It's by Tom Hadaway. About a North Shields fishing family.'

'Brilliant.'

'I think you could be in it,' he added slowly.

'What do you mean?'

'Well, it depends whether you want to turn professional,' he said.

It was a bombshell. It would mean jacking in my career at the shipyard in favour of turning professional. What followed was a cautious pep talk. Max told me he thought I had what it took but wanted me to think about it. He suggested we talk again in a few days and reluctantly I left it at that for the rest of the evening. It took a while to sink in and I couldn't pot a single ball once the proposition was in my head. It was the chance of a lifetime. Equity cards were like gold dust. Small touring theatre companies were given only two a year to hand out to new actors and I had a crack at one of them. It wasn't a difficult decision.

Two days later Ronan Patterson phoned, a director at the Northumberland Theatre Company. He'd seen me in *Bandits* and wanted to offer me a part in a play called *Operation Elvis.* It was another great part and, like *The Long Line,* would mean getting my hands on an Equity card. Either it was coincidence or I had reached a certain point in the north-east where people were starting to take notice.

When I phoned Max to tell him I'd had another offer he was taken aback. 'You're not doing it, are you?' he almost whispered. He was offering me the opportunity of a lifetime and it was inconceivable that I might be considering turning it down. In fact, that was never the problem. All I really needed was reassurance and a firm commitment.

Max asked me to come round for a chat. As I thought, his offer was rock solid and he had just wanted to give me space to think. He was older than me and already established in his career. Moving from youth theatre to professional theatre was a natural progression, but for me he knew it was different. I would be abandoning a steady career at the worst possible time, and with no cash to fall back on. Max knew I was hungry for the chance and capable of making the most it, but he took his responsibilities seriously and while he wanted to sound encouraging, he didn't want to push me.

'If you do go ahead with this,' he said finally, 'it's the most insecure profession you could choose. You'll have some good times and you'll take some hammerings, but I think you'll survive. Financially there will be no guarantees, but there's something about you that means you will work, even if it's only a few plays a year. I think you've got what it takes and I'd love you to do *The Long Line.*'

That was good enough for me.

I told Mam first and let her tell Dad. By the time he heard about it, the deed was done: I'd given in my notice at the shipyard. He says now that it's proof I've got a lucky streak, since although no one knew it at the time, the shipyards were only a few years from closure. But it's far easier to be philosophical with the benefit of hindsight. My dad had been immensely proud when I got the job at Swan Hunter and even if he didn't say so at the time, he must have been disappointed when I packed it in. If my mam was worried she didn't show it. She prides herself on leaving all of us to live our own lives and never discouraged me from leaving the job. As far as she was concerned, I was in charge of making my own decisions and I knew what I was doing.

My departure from Swan Hunter coincided with leaving home. Mam was losing another one and that probably upset her more than my leaving the shipyard. But she knew I was decisive. When the time came I just turned up one day and said, 'I'm leaving home on Saturday.' It was the same with the shipyard and the series of career moves I made over the years. Like my dad, I don't like looking back.

CHAPTER FIVE

At twenty-one I moved into a flat with Steve Chambers, a writer. Steve had previously run the Wallsend Youth Theatre while Max ran ours in Backworth. Both came under the same umbrella of Northern Arts, so we went to watch each other's shows and sometimes shared workshops.

Steve and I first came across each other when Joe Caffrey and I were in *Bandits* but met again at Max's one weekend for a night of cards and drinking. Steve was living nearby and I needed somewhere to sleep over, so I stayed at his place that night. When Steve moved to Heaton shortly after, he needed a lodger and I needed a room. We got on well and his flat was handy for the Corner House: straight along the Heaton

THE LONG LINE

Road and right at the Pork Shop and you were there. I was just starting work as a professional at the Live Theatre it and it seemed the right time to make the break from home.

It was my first flat and I treated poor Steve like a substitute parent. I made a mess; Steve tidied up. I did all those annoying things that non-flat-trained teenagers do: I left things where they dropped, woke him in the middle of the night when I'd forgotten my keys and drove him to distraction by regularly leaving the bathroom looking as if it had been hit by a flood. Years later I sent him a postcard with a still of Jack Nicholson in *One Flew Over the Cuckoo's Nest*. The actor was grinning insanely with a hose in his hand and I stuck on my own speech bubble: 'So this is how the bathroom got so wet.' I'm happy to say it still has pride of place on the wall above Steve's desk.

Needless to say, household economy was the last thing on my mind. I don't think Steve liked being cast in the role of Mr Sensible, but I left him no choice. Occasionally he'd tackle me, prompting parent-child-style conversations.

'Robson. When I came home today the door was wide open and the fire was full on.'

'It wasn't me.'

'But Robson, there's only you and me here.' Silence.

'Well, if you happen to see whoever it was, would you please ask them not to do it again.'

'Right.'

Steve came from Nottingham but, like many students who come to Newcastle to study, he ended up staying. He liked the feel of the city and particularly admired the way Newcastle celebrated its working-class traditions, in comparison with more the more bourgeois Nottingham, which seemed ashamed of its own. Whatever the reasons, he settled and made his life there.

Steve was a decade older than me, but despite the age difference we found ourselves in very similar circumstances at the time I moved in. After gaining a degree in mathematics, Steve earned a living as a computer programmer but had always written plays. Now, just as I was leaving the shipyard to start acting full time, Steve was giving up his job in computers to take his chances as a full-time playwright.

It gave the atmosphere a bit of an edge. We were excited and optimistic but also well aware of the risks attached to our professions. According to Steve, I seemed unworried by the urgency to earn, spending most of my time romancing women and lying around playing Billy Bragg songs on the guitar. He was far more industrious and was generally busy writing, perched eccentrically in an old dentist's chair and wearing his favourite fedora. When we got bored we got juvenile. We both did impressions and David Coleman was a favourite: 'And Green comes out of the bedroom, and yes, he's up early.' We did it all the time. At one point it got so bad we kept it up for two days without pause and ended up having to call a truce.

The Long Line was my first play as a professional, and it was to prove a turning point. The genius behind it was Tom Hadaway, who had started his working life in the fishing industry, running a couple of net boats out of North Shields. It was a thriving industry in those days and he built a good living out of it. As he approached his forties he felt financially stable enough to start to write and by chance found the idea to start him off.

Tom's first story came out of something that happened on the quayside one morning when a coble (a small fishing boat) came in to land its catch. In among the salmon and smaller fish was a live porpoise. Caught in the nets and thrashing around on the quay gasping for air, it caught the sympathy of a few fishermen, Tom among them, and together the men managed to get it back into the water. Because of the damage they do to nets, porpoises are usually unpopular with fishermen, but a cheer went up across the quay as it swam off into the river and spouted a triumphant farewell. It was a small slice of life but Tom thought it was worth putting down on paper and submitted it to the *Manchester Guardian* as a news item. It went in and, after capturing the public's interest, was reprinted in *Reader's Digest* and eventually made into a radio play which Tom read himself. As he tells it, his kids left the room in

embarrassment at the sound of their father's voice on the radio, thinking he was making a fool of himself. In fact, his instinctive feel for a story with something real and simple to say about people's lives was spot on and the porpoise story was only the first of many.

Tom took his inspiration from his friend and mentor, the playwright Cecil (C.P.) Taylor, who said: 'There's nay point in writin' anything unless ye have something to say.' It may sound blindingly obvious, but people write for all kinds of reasons, with varying degrees of success. 'Some people write because it's an appealing way to earn a living,' says Tom, 'better than working on a roof, ploughing a field or catching fish. But if you write because you have something to say about what you see around you – the people you know, the things that have happened in your life – the other qualifications will follow.' It's an over-modest self-assessment, but there's certainly a basic truth there which has guided his work since.

Spurred on by his initial success, Tom went on writing and a few years later travelled to Edinburgh with Cecil to see a production by radical playwright John McGraw's Theatre Sixty. The two new writers came back inspired and a fortnight later formed the Northeast Playwrights Society, modelled on a Scottish playwrights' society formed by McGraw. By this time Tom had received a BAFTA (British Association of Film and Television Arts) nomination for a play about his Uncle Jack, *God Bless You Jackie Maddison*. It was decided that if they were to take themselves seriously, members would have to have something of a track record. At that time, he recalls, they were a tight, elite group of only six, including himself and Cecil – which gives some indication of how hard it was to find acclaim as a writer in the north.

Tom started writing for the Live Theatre when it was first set up and later supported Max's candidacy for director when the vacancy came up in 1985. I first met him when we worked together on *Francie Nichol*. He had written the script and was very taken with the terrific enthusiasm of the youth theatre crowd. The following year we met again when I was asked to work with him on *The Long Line*.

The first read-through was like torture. I was the new boy and thrown together with people I regarded as great northern actors – Sammy Johnson, Val McLane, Annie Orwin, Denise Bryson and Dave Whittaker – I fluffed even the simplest lines. I knew the others vaguely but it was only Sammy that I knew really well. We often met for a drink at his house in Heaton. It was called The Triangle, partly because there was a little triangle of Christmas lights in the window but mainly because people went in for marathon parties and never came out.

Over the rehearsal period Tom and I developed a strong friendship. Writers aren't always welcomed at theatre rehearsals, but at the Live Theatre they were part of the whole process, and Tom's encouragement was very important to me. For one thing, our friendship was based on mutual respect for each other's work – although I was very much the beginner – but beyond that we just liked each other. Tom enjoyed working with young people and I was determined to inject into the wonderful play he had written the same energy that had first drawn him to youth theatre.

We opened at the Live Theatre in the summer of 1986. It was 16 July, the day of the Tall Ships Race in Newcastle, and the show was opened by Bobby Thompson, one of the greatest comics that ever lived even though he is little known outside the north-east. He was a huge draw in the clubs, and you couldn't move when he was playing, so it was quite a coup to get him. The critics were in on opening night, but even more nerve-racking, my parents, sisters, brother and Nana Sarah were all in the front row.

I needn't have worried. Our confidence in Tom's play was borne out by the audience's reaction. It went down a storm, and when we raced for the papers the following day we found the critics were equally impressed. Tom's fine writing was heaped with praise, Max was credited with 'rejuvenating' the Live Theatre and, to my amazement, I was even singled out. 'Green for Go' read one headline, while another critic claimed he couldn't take his eyes off 'this marvellously inventive actor'. I had worried that I was out of my depth alongside the others, yet the critics were pleased with the

'new blood' and wrote kindly that I 'looked fully at home in their company'.

I knew that what we were presenting made sense to the audience because it mirrored their own lives or their neighbours'. It was fine, intelligent theatre but also accessible entertainment, and this was proved when we later toured to packed pubs and clubs. When we played the piece at Ashington Social Club, we were on after a club singer, but among a rowdy audience of five hundred you could have heard a pin drop.

The level of praise we received for the play, and as individual actors, gave me a lot of confidence and gave my family something to be going on with. Mam had seen me in everything I'd done and her reaction was always the same: 'Eee, you were marvellous.' But for all that she hadn't really believed it was more than a hobby until *The Long Line*. Now the papers were writing about me, what they were saying was great and Mam knew it wasn't just a mother's bias. Dad loved it too and still says it's the best thing I ever did. It was the first real production he'd ever seen me in outside school and although he wouldn't admit it, I think it came as a complete surprise to him that I could act.

On a personal level it confirmed what I believed about theatre: the best plays are about ordinary people and the way they relate to each other. *The Long Line* is a brilliant slice of social history, but above all it is driven by relationships, and nearly everything I've done since has been the same.

The Long Line also made a big impression on someone else: Alison Ogilvie, a student of textiles and design at Manchester Polytechnic. Homesick for Newcastle, she heard an actor whose name she didn't catch reading the play for radio, and found it so evocative she cried. It was a few years before we would meet and eventually marry.

After the success of *The Long Line* I was on a high and completely unprepared for the unemployment that followed. In the greater scheme of things, three or four months without work was a very short time but it didn't feel that way. I was straining at the leash and didn't know when I'd work again or even whether I'd work again. 'If it all goes pear-shaped, there's a place for you at the shipyards,' my boss at Swan Hunter, Bill Crackett, had always said. But I hadn't expected to find myself recalling his words so soon.

I had been given the gift of a great part, the reviews had followed and I hadn't expected the momentum to stop. My confidence had always been what had kept me going, but suddenly I had no work and, for the first time, nothing to fall back on. It was my first experience of the feelings of insecurity notorious among actors. As an actor all you have to blame is yourself, because it's all you have: it's your machinery.

When I was low it didn't show. I know how depressed I was about being unemployed after *The Long Line*, but those who saw most of me at that time remember it differently. Both Steve and my mam remember me being in high spirits, as always. I guess everybody has a role within their family. Dawn was the boss, David the shy one and Joanna the sensible one. I was the entertainer, more emotional and more likely to cry or lose my temper temporarily, but generally the one who kept everyone laughing. Once cast in that role, I guess I was always perceived that way and maybe I kept playing the part even when it didn't fit.

Luckily I had people around me who could lend me a few quid and Steve did, again and again, despite the fact that he was struggling to earn a living himself. To make things worse, I would come back from the theatre or the pub absolutely slaughtered on a tenner he'd lent me and steal all his grub from the fridge. Anything I could lay my hands on was fair game and he became very resourceful at hiding food from me, even taking to stashing the previous night's leftovers in the cupboard where he kept his tools. Fortunately, I'd learned to cook from Nana Sarah and occasionally I would make amends by splashing out half my dole money and serving up something lavish that neither of us could really afford.

By day, Steve would be typing away and I'd sit and watch TV to take my mind off work, or the lack of it. He thought I was a lazy sod, but my story was that it was research. I wasn't just watching telly, I assured him from a reclining position on the sofa: I was studying it and picking up tips from the actors. I don't suppose he believed me, but there was actually a lot of truth in it. I loved films and never missed Paul Newman in older movies like *Cat on a Hot Tin Roof* and *Cool Hand Luke*. It was Newman's 'less is more' approach that I admired. His eyes were the key: so intense that he could convey thoughts and emotions almost without words. Although more physical, Brando had the same intensity and his combination of machismo and sensitivity was unique. There was no limit to the times I could watch and rewind scenes from *On the Waterfront*, *The Wild*

One and *A Streetcar Named Desire*. At the other end of the spectrum were Laurel and Hardy films: brilliant comedies but also beautifully poignant. The plots were unimportant; what really mattered was the friendship between the plaintive, over-emotional Stan and the pompous, overbearing Ollie. I absorbed it all like a sponge and stored it away for future use, just as I had throughout my childhood. It took me back to the days when the telly was new and the Hudson boys came calling.

'I see you've got the telly on,' Keith would start.

'Aye.'

'What's on?' Colin would chip in.

'Laurel and Hardy. The one where Laurel gets his head trapped between the side of a boat's hull and the mast and he's trying to saw himself free while Ollie is busy paintin' the top of the mast.'

'Oh yeah,' they'd both laugh. 'That one's a belter.'

'Aye.'

'Can we come in then?'

'No.'

Watching the box was instructive, but it didn't find me work or pay the bills. Towards the end I was so desperate I thought I'd try my hand at writing. I spent a lot of time walking round the Dene, the local park, looking to nature for inspiration, but after a few weeks spent gazing out the window from Steve's old dentist's chair, creating whimsical intros – 'The blossom fluttered on to the lonely streets...' – and filling the bin with failed attempts, I realized there were some things I should leave to Steve.

Bits and pieces came in, but not everything was on a par with *The Long Line*. In 1986 I made a brief appearance as Pete the Metro Man, which would have been more memorable if they'd used the first take. It was a TV and poster campaign to raise awareness of vandalism on the Newcastle Metro and my big line – well, my only line – was: 'It's your Metro, kids – look after it.' For that I was to earn a whacking £1500. The only problem was, I got so excited at the prospect of having a bit of cash that I went straight out and spent half of it getting slaughtered – the night before the shoot. Maybe it was the bags under my eyes the size of suitcases, or maybe it was my slurred delivery, but they were not impressed and the whole thing had to be reshot at great expense the following day.

Generally, it was a waiting game – not something I'm suited to. Fed up with waiting for the phone to ring, I started hassling my agent, Dave Holley, who had mostly strippers and magicians on his books. Miraculously, he managed to come up with a glimmer of hope. London's New Vic were casting *The Hunchback of Notre Dame*. I hopped on the next clipper and headed south. I was auditioned for the part of Pierre, 'ze best swordsman in all of France' and I figured my best bet was to make it funny. Hamming it up for all I was worth in a French accent to outdo Charles Aznavour, I gave it my best shot. Seven deadpan faces stared up from the empty auditorium as I juggled my blade dangerously and frantically rolled my r's. The silence was deafening. No one needs to tell you when you haven't got a part. You just know.

The horizon looked bleak. In acting the first question is always 'What are you doing next?' and I didn't have anything to say. I was living on lentil soup, making my own bread and, to make things worse, Shelley and I were drifting apart. Our separate careers in singing and acting were taking us in different directions and it was becoming harder and harder to sustain the relationship. At the same time I was beginning to wonder if the whole acting dream had been a ridiculous mistake when Max came to the rescue.

He was putting together an a cappella musical called *Scrap* and he knew I could sing. There were five female parts and one male; it was mine if I wanted it. Unusually, the play hadn't been commissioned by Max, which should have warned me of things to come. It was work, but suffice to say the review in the *Stage* simply put a line through the 'S' of the title. They tore it to pieces and somewhere along the line we realized they were right. The music was fantastic, the singing was beautiful, but the play was a turkey. Despite the chilly reception, we had to finish the run because it was subsidized. The worst moments came when we toured with it. On a good night we pulled in an audience of ten or twelve, and one desperate night in Rook Hill, Glasgow, we played to a solitary woman who refused our pleas to refund her money and demanded that we perform. It was a real dignity stripper.

Thankfully, better things were round the corner. *Kidder's Luck* was a breath of fresh air. It was a lovely book written by Jack Common and adapted for the stage by Phil Woods (now a writer for

JOE CAFFREY AND I IN *KIDDER'S LUCK* AT THE LIVE THEATRE, IN WHICH I PLAYED HIS FATHER.

Coronation Street) about a young man's attempts to change his life. I played the father and Great Uncle Alfie, and Joe Caffrey played Will Kidder, the lead. Will wants to escape his life of poverty. He aspires to material wealth and the status that he imagines will come with it, but he comes to realize that friendship and integrity must be sacrificed along the way. At the heart of the play is the conviction that a more compassionate, socialist approach to life is actually the way to find what Will is looking for. It was a beautifully crafted piece and we were happy to be working with material with which we identified so closely.

As John in *Hands*, **my first television part, for BBC North East.**

Apart from that it was great to be working with Joe. We got on as well as ever and were both facing the same kind of ups and downs in our careers. Always short of cash, we once decided to dress as racetrack inspectors and try to get into the Newcastle racecourse without paying. Dressed in brown anoraks and trilbys, we strolled about prodding the course expertly and shouting the odd 'Good but firm' to each other. Sure enough, we got in, laid bets on five horses and lost everything. I think the last horse I backed is still running.

Kidder's Luck went down well, was fun to do and opened up another door just when I needed it. In the audience were director Corrine Campbell Hill and producer Ruth Caleb, who were sufficiently impressed to offer me an audition for the part of Rick in a BBC1 play called *A Night on the Tyne*.

At that point my only TV experience – apart from Pete the Metro Man, of course – had been a TV play for BBC North East called *Hands*. This was the work of Newcastle writer Sid Chaplin, a former miner who wrote stories about miners and their lives. It was a very moving story about a father and son who work side by side in the mines but have stopped speaking to each other after an argument. When a rock fall leaves them trapped underground, the son finally breaks the silence and begins to tell his father how much he loves him, not realizing his father has been fatally injured.

I was cast as the son by director Mark Scrimshaw, who had seen me in *The Long Line*, and Tim Healy played the father. It was a beautiful story, but it was made on a tiny budget of £6000. With its wobbly sets and cut-price locations, I knew it had no chance of a national screening, but the story's integrity and Tim's friendship made it a wonderful experience. Perhaps because the audience was small and local, I wasn't particularly nervous but *A Night on the Tyne* was a different ballgame. We were talking network TV.

I read the script and really liked it. By complete coincidence, it is about four Geordie shipyard workers – so I was on familiar territory – and takes place as the yards are in the process of being dismantled. Faced with redundancy, the four men launch a ship in the middle of the night

as a last defiant stand. In fact, it was loosely based on an incident that occurred at Swan Hunter.

The producers got in touch with David Holley and I was called to the audition in Newcastle. I felt it went well, but they were unsure and told me they couldn't make up their minds, although they had narrowed it down to a choice between me and another actor, Steve Tompkinson (who went on to appear in *Ballykissangel, Drop the Dead Donkey* and *Brassed Off*). A second audition followed, this time in Dave Holley's offices. Again the producers went away looking happy but still didn't reach a decision. Once again they said they would get in touch. I wasn't sure what else I could do.

They called and asked to see me again the next day. This time I was really at a loss. My nerves were frayed. I couldn't work out what they wanted and went in prepared to tackle them about the need for a third audition. In the event it wasn't necessary. They offered me the part. It was a tremendous relief and, as usual, I started spending the money the next day.

It was a one-hour play and I was acting alongside Alun Armstrong, who was an absolute hero to me. There have been moments in my life which took me in a certain direction and watching Alun in *Get Carter*, when I was about nine, was one of them. The film is an English gangland picture, loosely based on the Angus Sibbet murder and, to my amazement as a kid raised mainly on the American equivalent, it was shot in Newcastle. There was Alun with this Geordie accent I could identify with, but he wasn't playing a token Geordie: he was a three-dimensional character accessible to everyone. I sat perched on the edge of my seat, taking it all in. In the back of my mind was one clear thought: maybe I can do this. I'd grown up Alun's greatest fan and now I was acting alongside him. It made me feel that anything was possible. Until we started filming, that is.

By the time filming began I was sick with nerves. The first scene might as well have been dreamed up by a sadist with a grudge against actors. Rick, my character, is a shipyard apprentice but has dreams of making it as a magician in London and spends most of his spare time practising his act. In the first scene I had to stand in a tower-block window overlooking the Tyne and *juggle* as the shot was filmed from a helicopter. It was an ambitious, two-minute opening shot which involved the helicopter swooping up the bend of the river, passing North Shields, Swan Hunter and Vickers Armstrong, moving ever closer to the top floor of the tower block and eventually homing in on the window where I stood juggling. If acting while juggling was a challenge, the sight of two tons of helicopter simultaneously screaming to within a few feet of my face was more than I could deal with. I was sweating buckets, the balls were slipping through my hands and I had a strong suspicion I was going to vomit before anyone had a chance to call 'Action'. I knew full well that it was costing a fortune and that I had a look of frozen terror on my face, but I couldn't shift it, and the screams of

WITH TIM HEALY (FAR RIGHT) AND MARK SCRIMSHAW, THE DIRECTOR OF *HANDS*.

REHEARSAL BREAK DURING
THE FILMING OF *A NIGHT ON
THE TYNE* FOR BBC1. FROM
LEFT: ALUN ARMSTRONG,
LESLIE SCHOFIELD, ME AND
BRIAN PRINGLE.

of day, I wasn't replaced. As it turned out, I wasn't the only beginner on set, and that may have saved my bacon. At one point, as the four men launch the boat, Rick has to leap into the air, punching out in triumph. We tried it several times, but they just weren't happy with the shot. 'Robson,' the director shouted suddenly, as if inspiration had struck. 'When you jump into the air, could you just hold it there a little bit longer?' I think that's when I realized I wasn't the only one who didn't know what they were doing.

Once we got into the swing of things it got easier. I learned quickly to look to the more experienced actors for tips and Alun Armstrong was a great role model, just as Tim Healy had been on *Hands*. I also got to know the whole crew. I could see we were all in it together and it struck me how odd it would be to be one of those actors who isolates himself in his trailer and emerges two minutes before his shot. I realized that the more I under-

'Robson, for Christ's sake, relax!' which surfaced over the din of the helicopter engines did nothing to help. Takes two, three, four, five, six and seven were no better. It was a bad first day and I spent that night in a cold sweat trying to resign myself to the fact that I simply couldn't do the job. I was sure to be fired and I went over the scenario in my head. They would probably try to break it to me gently, tell me I wasn't playing the part as they had envisaged it and that I would be paid for my work so far but replaced.

Although the opening scene never saw the light

stood the craft of the director of photography and camera operators, the better the end result would be. I bought myself a book on cameras and the way they worked, poring over diagrams of long lenses and wide-angle lenses, picking up on techniques I thought I could use. I learned how to focus on somebody by looking into their right eye. I read that an actor's eyes can look very different on screen, depending on what he is wearing. A white shirt, for example, lifts blue eyes – a vital tip for a blue–eyed boy like myself who as a kid had modelled himself on Paul Newman. All I had to do was combine camera technique with the one guiding rule I had learned in theatre: be honest. Put the truth in it and play the emotion.

If I could do that, I figured, I could just about survive my first taste of TV.

CHAPTER SIX

Before I knew it I was unemployed again, smoking too much and trying not to worry about where my next job was coming from. *A Night on the Tyne* was great experience but I'd always known that, no matter how good, a play about four shipyard workers and the impact of unemployment was unlikely to set the world on fire. That's just the way of things.

It whetted my appetite for television, though. It may have been an arduous learning curve with plenty of sleepless nights, but I'd loved every minute of it. There was also the money. Theatre's a great experience, but you've got to eat. Michael Caine once put it in a nutshell. Already a big star, he was invited to do a prestigious piece of theatre,

TRYING IT AND LIKING IT

for which he was offered £500 a week. 'Why would I want to do that?' he asked. 'Because,' the answer came back, 'it's Art.' His response was crass but realistic. 'I've just made six million on a film and I bought a Picasso – *that's* fuckin' art.' He's dead right. Great parts are fantastic, but after a few years struggling on £50 a week I knew I couldn't live on theatre wages for ever.

I decided to head for the smoke. I figured I might be better placed to find work and I wanted to catch up with Shelley. She was working in London as a singer and living in Palmers Green, which is where I was planning to kip. It was the only time I lived in London, and I hated it. As it turned out, it was too late to rescue the relationship with Shelley – I later found out she

IN *BLACKBERRY TIME* AT THE LIVE THEATRE WITH DAVID WHITTAKER.

was already seeing someone else – but I was in the right place for work. Out of the blue Dave Holley rang me. He'd been contacted by one of the country's top casting agents, Jane Arnell, who told him the BBC were doing open auditions for *Casualty*. The part of a porter was up for grabs and they wanted a regional character.

There had already been two series of *Casualty*, but at that time it was by no means established as a success. Politically it was very sparky, dealing head on with issues that were hitting the Health Service. After a disappointing first series the BBC intended to drop it, but luckily for me it was given a second chance when the producer, Geraint Morris, managed to convince them that it could work if the scripts were right. (Sadly, Geraint Morris died during the writing of this book.)

At the audition I met Peter Norris, the producer, and Jane Arnell. Needless to say, I was shit-scared,

but Jane seemed to like me and with her was the director, Andrew Morgan, who had seen me in a play called *Blackberry Time* at the Live Theatre and liked it. It was a good start. I knew he was batting for me, but this also meant there were expectations to meet.

After an initial reading I was recalled to do a screen test with Vivienne McKone, the extremely attractive actress with whom my character was having a on-screen relationship. After the audition I headed back to Shelley's place to wait for the news and when it came I could barely believe it. Andrew and Peter were unsure – the story of my life – and were trying to decide between me and another actor. It was bloody Steve Tompkinson again. I was called a third time, and tried to boost my confidence by telling myself that Andrew was fighting my corner. Then, drained by anticipation, I headed back to Newcastle to wait for the news.

I'd missed home and if I'd learned anything

over the last few months it was that I would never live in London again. I just couldn't connect with it. I'd been shocked by the poverty gap, the run-aways sleeping outside tube stations, the racist cabbies and the jingoism that exists in the south. I'd longed for the warmth of Newcastle and was glad to get back to Steve Chambers's place. There was one other thing I'd learned: never trust drummers. The relationship with Shelley was over and I'd lost out to one of the boys in the band.

I was playing pool in the Corner House when the message came through to call Dave Holley and within a few minutes he was telling me I'd got the part. It was funny. I was drinking with a crowd of lads who'd all gone to drama school and there I was, a former shipyard apprentice who'd gone a completely different route, but I'd cracked it all

IN *BLACKBERRY TIME* AT THE LIVE THEATRE WITH JANE WADE.

53

the same. By an amazing fluke an actor called Eddie Nestor was also in the bar that night. He was a regular on *Casualty* and had heard on the grapevine that I'd got the part even before my agent did. He hadn't wanted to jump the gun, but now the news was out it was time to celebrate. 'How much they payin' you?' he asked. 'Fortunes,' I replied, already planning what to spend it on.

The part was a huge leap forward. It was mainstream, peak-time TV. Initially I was guaranteed twelve episodes, but it was a series with a future and it also meant serious money. It was even worth going back to London for.

First stop was the BBC studios in Acton, west London, where the read-throughs were to take place. Everything had moved so quickly and it was only as I walked from the tube that I realized how nervous I felt. I was on my way to the rehearsal rooms where countless programmes had been made, programmes I'd been mesmerized by as a kid. I was on the verge of entering a world I'd only watched from the outside and I was terrified. If I failed, I would be out as suddenly as I'd arrived and I might not get another chance.

As I approached the zebra crossing that took me across to the studios I saw a flash-looking car steaming towards me. It always pissed me off that Londoners were in too much of a hurry to stop, and determined to call his bluff, I stepped out on to the black and white lines. The shiny Jag screeched to an angry halt and I caught sight of the face at the window. It was David Jason. *David*

THE CAST FROM MY FIRST SERIES OF *CASUALTY*. ON THE FAR LEFT, NIGEL LE VAILLANT, ON THE FAR RIGHT, PATRICK ROBSON.

Jason. As it hit me that we were filming next door to *Only Fools and Horses*, I realized I was as starstruck as any kid.

From there on in things just got worse. I headed straight for the canteen for a quick coffee to calm my nerves only to find I was queuing alongside Una Stubbs, Joan Plowright, Stephen Fry and Hugh Laurie, Patrick McGoohan, John Gielgud and what looked like the entire cast of *EastEnders*. It was a struggle to stop my head from swivelling and my jaw from dropping. These were actors I'd grown up with, some of whom had had profound influences on my life through the TV. I was completely overawed by the whole thing and we hadn't even started filming yet.

The read-throughs passed in a blur, but by the time we moved to Bristol, where *Casualty* was filmed, I was feeling slightly more comfortable. Most of our time was spent hanging about in the green room waiting for our scenes. It was small and cramped, a bit bigger than a caravan, and always smelled vaguely of the sandwiches that arrived at regular intervals on huge trays. When we were called, we went through a set of plastic doors which from the other side were part of the set. It was a surreal experience. As you emerged through the doors you left the hospitality room and entered what looked and felt like a real, functioning hospital ward.

The schedule was very intensive, and those first days of filming were excruciating. I felt completely out of my depth. Stress is a drawback of any job, but as an actor there is no way to disguise it; it affects your every move. In the early days of *Casualty* the smallest scene involving the most everyday behaviour – crossing a room and picking up a cup, say – became the most unnatural and complicated manoeuvre. Then there was the bloody trolley. It hadn't occurred to me as I learned my lines that whenever Jimmy the porter appeared a trolley with a mind of its own would be leading the way. I was lumbered with that trolley for three years and at the end it was still the trolley that was in control.

With my body behaving as randomly as the trolley and a first scene which involved making small talk with the receptionist – the distractingly gorgeous Vivienne – I was painfully aware of my every move. I knew that what I was committing to celluloid would be seen by a lot of people and although I was constantly reassured that I could get it wrong and go again, I still felt like the 'new boy' with something to prove. My dilemma seemed impossible to resolve. In order to act I couldn't hold anything back but in order to let go I had to be relaxed.

I've never spent a lot of time researching characters because it hasn't been necessary but for Jimmy I needed some understanding of what a porter's job involves: the daily routine as well as the technical side. Jimmy started life as a very sketchy outline but Peter wanted to develop the part and if I wanted to last beyond twelve episodes it was in my interests to help. With this in mind I spent some time in a hospital watching porters. What I quickly discovered was that they spend a lot of time waiting around – for patients who need moving, beds that need delivering, X-rays and blood samples that need picking up – and what they do while they wait is chat. They cruise the waiting rooms and wards chatting to nurses, anxious patients and their relatives and when they're not doing that they sit in the porters' lodge and natter over endless cups of tea. If you want to know anything in a hospital the porter will always have the low-down. While doctors were either unavailable or unapproachable, I realized it was often the porter that people turned to when they were scared, lonely or just bored.

I found it easiest to understand Jimmy in terms of his relationships with others. What's particularly interesting about porters is that they're often the first point of contact for a patient and the last. They bring patients in when they arrive and wheel them out to the ambulance when they've been discharged. Whatever journey that patient goes through – emotionally and physically – the porter is always there.

Jimmy's character began to take shape. We settled on the idea of a young guy with little formal education but a conscience and an opinion. Someone with deep-rooted ideas about the NHS, who has grown up believing people shouldn't pay for the misfortune of being ill – a socialist at heart without even realizing it. Like the best comic roles of classic theatre, he's the clown, but a clown with

TAKING A BREAK WITH PATRICK ROBINSON (ASH) ON THE SET OF CASUALTY.

some profound comments to make. Being allowed to develop my own character in this way was a great opportunity. Often a script is all sewn up by the time the actors come on the scene, but Peter Norris, one of the best producers I've worked with, was always open to my input. In time I was able to build up the character from a guy who pushed trolleys in the background to a complex figure, integral to life in the hospital.

Crucially, I was also able to ad lib and occasionally write my own lines, which probably saved me from getting the push. I was on really dodgy ground at the start and I knew it: there had been mutterings that I wasn't going to work out and that sort of talk gets back to you. I knew the reason I was failing was that I wasn't relaxed with the syntax. Certain lines and words were unnatural to

me, because of where I was born, but I didn't have the bottle to say it until the second or third episode. When I eventually asked if I could phrase some things differently I found it was no problem. The relief was enormous and so, I hope, was the change in my performance.

With a clearer idea of what Jimmy was about, and permission to put into his mouth words that I was comfortable with, I started to relax. Everything gradually fell into place and I could bring a lightness to the part, which was what they had wanted from the beginning. I could also start to enjoy it and get to know the cast better.

The BBC set me up in a series of shared flats in Bristol as they often do when actors are filming away from home. While I was waiting for the first one to be sorted out I stayed with Brenda Fricker, who played Megan in the show. There was a lot to learn during my first series of *Casualty* and Brenda was the one to watch. She's real through and through, and every nuance, every emotion and every line is totally believable. A year later I would sit watching telly in Brenda's front room as she made her way to the stage to pick up her Oscar for *My Left Foot*. It was a great night. Only days after being fêted from coast to coast, she was back to work on the set of *Casualty*. Brenda is nobody's fool and wasn't the type to have her head turned by the glamour and glitz of Hollywood. She's far too sharp. When a newspaper reported that 'the Irish actress had been seen drunk in an airport' she replied, 'When I'm drunk I'm an Irish actress but when I win the Oscar I'm a British actress.'

After briefly sharing a flat in Redcliffe with Vivienne McKone (scoring a big fat zero on the old points system), I moved in with Patrick Robinson, who was playing Ash in the series, and Nigel Le Vaillant, the lead in *Dangerfield*. It was a great period socially. We all got on well and spent a lot of time just enjoying one another's company and listening to Nigel telling stories. Nigel has a supreme intellect and reintroduced me to the kind of literature I'd felt so baffled by at school. Once you've been put off something as a child it's quite hard to come back to it, but Nigel could read poetry and Shakespeare in such a way that it was both lyrically beautiful and meaningful. Patrick and I could listen to him for hours.

His political knowledge also made a big impression on me. He was from a very different background and had studied political history at Oxford, so he came at things from quite a different perspective. Yet we had a lot in common and both got a lot of pleasure as we sat together and watched Geoffrey Howe give his resignation speech that year. He described Thatcher as the captain of a cricket team, sending her team out to the front line to bat, only to find their equipment was useless and their chances ruined. A cricketing metaphor might not have been my own first choice, but it was the most eloquent and heartfelt destruction imaginable of everything Thatcher stood for. We could see it was the beginning of the end for her; a year later came the leadership challenge and she was on her way out.

Naturally there was more to life than political debate and poetry reading. Patrick was a keen dancer and when we'd had enough of the telly we'd hit the local nightspots. I don't know anyone who can dance like Patrick who isn't actually making a living from it. Every woman in the place would have her eyes glued to him doing some fantastic funky thing – and he wouldn't even be trying. It would never be long, though, before their gaze would shift to the melk by his side. Maybe my own dancing style was just ahead of its time. It was certainly unique. Friends would just stare and shout, 'What the hell's that you're doing?' Girls would just stare but not for the reason they stared at Patrick. The worst mistake I could make would be to try to copy Patrick. I couldn't pull it off and looked even more ridiculous. While Patrick fought off the girls I got to choose my form of torture: the brief humiliation of sloping off versus the prolonged embarrassment of going on.

As we started the second series of *Casualty* my pay shot up to £1300 per episode, plus expenses because I was still based in Newcastle. I must have been the only actor on the payroll who didn't have a bank account and this bundle of money was going straight into my pocket. Sensible Steve stayed with me in Bristol around that time and was horrified to find stacks of coins and fivers lying all over the flat. He gave me a lecture on the rudiments of banking (and tidied up) before he left. Of course, he was dead right. Since my early days on the series I'd been getting through money like water down a drain. In those days most nights were spent at the Castle pub, next to the BBC rehearsal rooms, slowly getting slaughtered with Brenda, Derek Thompson and Vivienne. My first week's living expenses went fifty-fifty on booze and a flight home, my first real extravagance. I wasn't to be trusted with a pocketful of twenties, but there was something about it I liked.

I suppose I found cash reassuring after a childhood spent scrabbling around for fifty-pence pieces to feed the meter. It was something tangible I could hold in my hand which meant security – not just for me but for my family. For the first time I was going home at weekends able to say, 'Here, Mam', 'Here, Dad.' It was fantastic.

I grew more confident with the second series and the part continued to expand. Jimmy evolved into a character with his own story-lines, his own personal dilemmas. At my suggestion we also took on his life outside the hospital. He was a bit of a womanizer, a wide boy on the surface but underneath quite a lonely guy, whose pursuit of happiness was unfulfilling. It wasn't long before he'd become a mainstay of the series.

As Jimmy became more popular I started to get recognized, if only locally at first. No one ever called me Robson; it was always 'Jimmy'. 'Hey, Jimmy, I've got a bad finger,' was the usual, but my favourite was a young kid who came up to me in the street. 'Hey, Jimmy,' he called to get my attention. '*Needle-e nee-nee-nee, needle-e nee-nee-nee…*' He went on to 'needle-e' the entire *Casualty* signature tune, never the catchiest of theme tunes and a bastard to perform a cappella. I think I was as chuffed as he was.

I was with *Casualty* for three years and inevitably I started to get bored. But feeling bored and having the confidence to pack it in were two different things. To make things worse, the decision had to be made in advance. As is usual, I was asked at the start of the second series whether I wanted to do a third and I said no. It was a leap in the dark – the money had been good, the work regular and in the meantime I'd met Ali.

CHAPTER SEVEN

Our first 'date' was at the Quay Club in Newcastle's Dean Street. I was due to meet my friends Karen and Andrew, and Karen had told me she was bringing a friend along. I knew nothing about her except that she and Karen had met at Manchester Polytechnic, where they were both studying textiles and design. As I approached the club I could see no sign of Karen and Andrew, but I spotted someone waiting alone, shifting restlessly from foot to foot in her black Doc Martens. She was about five foot five with a mane of long, brown hair, a black miniskirt and a lovely pair of pins. Was this Karen's friend? I hoped it was. I introduced myself. Her name was Alison and she had the most beautiful hazel eyes I'd ever seen. Karen

SAD GOODBYES AND NEW BEGINNINGS

and Andrew were obviously late, so the two of us went into the club.

The place was packed but the dance floor was empty and Tom Jones's *It's Not Unusual* was blaring out of the speakers. I decided to go for it. The way I saw it, any woman who'd take to the floor with old snake-hips Green must be OK.

Our relationship was definitely a slow burner and we went out with friends for a long time before I finally asked her out properly. The more I saw of Ali the more I liked her. When we met up we talked non-stop and for once *my* job wasn't the subject of conversation. Instead, we talked about her work. Although she was studying during the day, in the evenings she was working with people with cerebral palsy. At that stage it was voluntary work, but a few years later she would abandon textiles to make it her career. It was a world I knew nothing about and for once I found myself talking and thinking about something other than acting.

Actors, and that's who I was seeing most of, tend to talk all the time about themselves and their work, and I was no exception. There's a certain egocentricity in being an actor, but then without it you wouldn't have the bottle to get yourself on to the stage. By contrast, Ali's job was all about putting her ego to one side and caring for other people. While the most important part of my week might be learning a script or poring over the ratings, she was fighting to get wheelchair ramps into discos, disabled access to pubs, working with people up against fantastic odds and changing their lives in the most direct of ways. It was refreshing, eye-opening and put acting in its place.

We saw each other often, but always seemed to end up as part of a group. One day I dropped in to visit her at work. She was going to the pub that night with a crowd from her workplace and asked if I wanted to come. It came as a shock when I realized 'the crowd' were all in wheelchairs, many severely disabled, but it didn't seem to have crossed Ali's mind. As far as she was concerned, there was absolutely no reason why people in wheelchairs shouldn't go down to the pub and get

blasted just like anyone else, because they were just like anyone else. And she was right. It was a great night and I knew I wanted to see Ali again, but alone next time.

TAKING IT *VERY* EASY WITH ALI AT OUR HOUSE IN TYNEMOUTH DURING A RARE BREAK BETWEEN JOBS.

At that time she was sharing a flat with three friends in inner-city Bishops Road, and I needed a way in. I settled on a plan of action and phoned to try it out. It wasn't original and it certainly wasn't the most romantic chat-up line she'd ever heard, but it worked a treat.

'Hiya, Ali.'

'Hi.'

'My TV's on the blink… Any chance of coming round and watching yours?'

'No problem.'

For the first time in my life I wasn't remotely interested in what was on the box and when the time came to order a cab home my heart skipped a beat as Ali whispered, 'I love you, you know.' Had it been someone else I would have jumped at the chance, but this was different. I felt more strongly about Ali than I had ever felt about anyone else and I was scared. Scared of the power of those feelings and the implications. Falling in love hadn't been part of my plans. I took a cab home.

Of course, there's no point trying to fight against falling in love. After that night we started to spend more time alone with each other. We both loved the quiet beauty of Northumberland's countryside and we'd often go walking in the hills together. Spending time with Ali and the people she worked with had a cumulative effect on me. Pontificating about scheduling and sub-plots seemed absurd set against what she was doing. Why am I getting so uptight about learning a script? I started to think.

Ali had a combination of strength, independence and compassion that I found very appealing. She was also the perfect counterpoint to my all-cylinders-firing hyperactivity, and I knew she was good for me.

The small step from closeness to intimacy was inevitable and a New Year's Eve party at her place was when it all came together. Spurred on by the party spirit and a few pints of plonk, I made my move. It was a turning-point in my life, but it's the details I remember. She was wearing a black shirt with white spots and I suddenly thought she was the most gorgeous creature I'd ever seen. Within days Ali turned up at my place in her black VW Beetle and asked if she could stay over. 'Yes,' I told her. 'Good,' said Ali. Until then I'd done all the running, but now I knew the die was cast.

After that new year I quickly became a regular fixture at Ali's flat in Bishops Road. As soon as filming ended in Bristol I'd be on the first train home. Ali was still on a student grant, having decided to take a second degree and train as an occupational therapist, and not long after we started going out with each other I asked to borrow £60 to pay my electric bill. That was a lot of money for someone on a grant and years later she joked that it was then she knew we were really serious.

Our lives fell into two distinct parts: Monday to Friday we went our separate ways and worked; weekends we were together for forty-eight hours. When I was short of cash I took advantage of the weekly train trip paid for by the BBC and on Friday nights Ali would pick me up in her car from the central station. However, if we were feeling flush I would rent a car in Bristol, turning up at Ali's place at three or four in the morning to find her waiting anxiously at the window.

Sometimes she would book us into a B&B and we'd head out of town until I had to go rushing off again on Sunday. If I could only manage to get home during the week, I would, and we would meet in her lunch-hour and head for the beach. Ali would go back to college with a big grin on

her face and sand in her hair. Gradually we realized that something that had begun so slowly had rapidly picked up speed. Our weekends together were great but we both wanted to move things on a stage. I loved Ali and for the first time I found I wanted to set up home with someone. Slowly we started to edge towards moving in together.

Although we already knew what we wanted, the impetus to do this came after an incident which brought everything into sharper perspective. Ali's flat was in a rough area where crime was commonplace and the streets were regularly lit up at night by police helicopters. She wasn't bothered but I worried about her, especially because I was away so much.

I was out that night having a drink in town with friends while Ali went to visit her sister. On her way home, not far from the flat, some kids smashed a brick through the passenger window of her car and grabbed her bag. Ali isn't a panicker and it was only once she got home that she realized how shaken up she was. Locked out because the flat keys were in the bag and without money to even make a phone call, she sat in the Beetle with the wind blowing through the shattered window until I came home. When I first jumped out of the taxi I couldn't work out what had happened. Ali was very cool, but when it

ALI AND I TAKE THE FAMOUS BLACK BEETLE FOR A SPIN NEAR HER HOME TOWN OF ASHINGTON, NORTHUMBERLAND.

sank in that she had actually been in the car when it was broken into, I realized I never wanted her to be so vulnerable again. If I needed a push, this was it.

I'd met Ali's mam and dad before we were officially going out and now the time came to introduce her to my family. Their first reaction was surprise, because she wasn't involved in acting, as previous girlfriends had tended to be, but my mam knew immediately that this one was serious. As usual, I presented things as a *fait accompli*, telling Mam after that first meeting that we wanted to get married and were going to look for a house.

I was more nervous about breaking the news to Ali's parents. Like me, she was very close to her mam and dad, and because she was the youngest of three daughters and the last to leave home, I knew her father would feel very protective towards her. We explained our plan – to live together for a year

SIGNING THE REGISTER AFTER THE WEDDING CEREMONY, ON 22 JUNE 1991, AT ST GEORGE'S LOCAL ECUMENICAL PROJECT CHURCH, ASHINGTON.

and then marry – and happily it went down well. Like any good father, he was a bit apprehensive about his daughter marrying an actor, but I did my best to reassure him. The truth was, my prospects didn't hold up well to scrutiny. I was in my last series of *Casualty*, with nothing lined up to follow it, and we needed a mortgage. I suspected it wouldn't be as easy to reassure the bank.

On paper it didn't look good. Ali was living on a student grant and not due to qualify for another year or so, while I was on the verge of becoming a 'resting' actor. I hadn't even had my own bank account until a few months earlier, when Ali had finally persuaded me to stop walking around town with my wages sticking out of my top pocket. We tried our luck at the Abbey National, figuring we might have more credibility because Ali banked there. Maybe I really am as lucky as my dad claims I am, because that's where I met Sandra, a financial adviser, who recognized me from *Casualty*.

She sorted out my financial life. For starters, she supported our application for a mortgage, a decision based purely on gut instinct. She was taking a big risk. I could have been straight back to theatre and £50 a week after *Casualty*, but for some reason she had confidence in both of us. So she got me the mortgage and I got myself a new accountant. Eight years later Sandra is still with me and has saved me from near disaster more than once.

By August 1990 Ali and I were the proud joint owners of our own place in Tynemouth. It was one of a row of Victorian maisonettes near to a stunning five-mile stretch of beach that I used to visit as a kid. As it turned out, it was also a house with a history. When the previous occupants moved out a couple of guys were hired to remove the rubbish. Ali and I had already come across all sorts of bizarre bits and pieces under the floorboards, including women's knickers and a collection of violent horror books, but when a human skeleton fell out of a bin bag, the removal guy nearly had a heart attack. Before we knew it, the police were on the doorstep and we found our new home was at the heart of a murder enquiry. There were red faces all round when it was later discovered that the skeleton was made of plaster.

We stayed in Tynemouth for five or six years,

although as I became more well known it got more difficult. Living opposite a secondary school didn't help and Ali had to get used to a constant stream of kids knocking on the door or peering through the kitchen window as she did the dishes. I never saw it as the place we'd settle down in anyway. I dreamed of living in the country, off a remote road, surrounded by trees and rolling hills, with a view so good it might even take my mind off the telly.

The time had come to push through the jelly doors to *Casualty* for the last time. I was going to miss the people I'd been working with for the best part of three years, but I needed to move on. In the end, Jimmy's exit was less than breathtaking. He said his goodbyes and left Holby General to become a factory driver delivering suits – hardly the unforgettable finale I'd hoped for. Even my

mam phoned to say, 'So is that it then? You're a driver for a factory?'. I suppose it was a way of leaving the door open for me to come back, although I had a feeling it wouldn't happen.

IN OUR GARDEN IN NORTHUMBERLAND WITH FERN.

The end of *Casualty* coincided with the end of another, more important part of my life. It was on the final day's filming for the final episode that Nana Sarah died. Ali was trying to get in touch all morning, leaving increasingly urgent messages, but I was in the middle of a major scene and no one could reach me on set. When I finally got a message to phone home immediately, I knew it was something terrible. It's the kind of message you dread. My nana had been ill for a while and although I suspected what the news might be, I didn't want to deal with it in front of everyone else.

At that time I was staying in Bristol with Patrick Robinson and his wife Janice, and rushed home to call from there. Ali had already contacted them and as soon as I stepped through the door their faces told me everything I needed to know. When someone close dies, there is no way you can rationalize the event, no way you can prepare yourself for the words you know are inevitable. When Ali told me Nana Sarah had died I just let the phone drop and collapsed in a heap. Janice held on to me as I cried.

I learned a lot from Nana Sarah and it seemed impossible to get used to the idea that I would never see her alive again. My dad had taken me to visit her shortly before she died and said afterwards he wished he hadn't because I got too upset. Old and tired though she was, she refused to give in. She had stroke after stroke but, like my dad, she seemed strong and somehow invincible. I had an image of her in my head from that day, shaking her fist at the heavens shouting, 'Is that the best you can do?' Now I was heading home for her funeral. I loved her and thanked God I'd told her so the last time I saw her.

It was a sad, sad day which began with a viewing at the house so that friends and family could say their goodbyes. I couldn't face it. I disliked the ritual and I didn't want to see my nana that way anyway. The part of Nana Sarah that mattered, that I had loved, the vibrancy and strength that I associated with her, was gone and I couldn't see the hope in it. When the funeral cortège came through the village, people came out and took off their caps as a mark of respect and at the church a woman cleric managed to celebrate Nana Sarah's character in a way that was neither cloying nor impersonal. I had been asked to read a poem, but I couldn't do it.

Watching her suffer had been terrible, but watching my dad deal with her death was almost worse. I'd never seen him this exposed. Seeing a grown man crumbling is somehow more unbearable because it's so rare. I knew too that there were a lot of things he hadn't said to his mother and now it was too late. For my dad it had never been easy to ask for help, but after Nana Sarah died there was a time when he would ring me at three in the morning just wanting to chat. I tried to make sure I saw more of him. In a reverse of the situation where I had felt safe at the fair with my hand in his, I wanted to hold his hand and give him some support.

Life goes on and I had plenty to take my mind off the sadness. Ali and I had married on 22 June 1991. We'd lived together before that, but I think it was a relief to both families when I made an honourable woman of her. As they say in the north-east, living together is 'a foot in the door to get out'.

The wedding was a sensational day. We didn't want anything too grand and married in a local church in Ashington. Ali had gone there as a child and it was the church where both her elder sisters, Gillian and Helen, had married, as had Ali's parents. Although neither of us is particularly religious, it was nice that there was a family connection.

It was as nerve-racking as a first night. All our mates were there and Joe Caffrey was best man, so we both had speeches to make. Joe said it was more like doing an audition, because many of my friends were actors. He brought the house down with a very moving speech that referred back to my mining heritage and childhood in the north-east. But he didn't get any work.

Dad was as proud as Punch and was delighted to be introduced to Tim Healy, a friend and local actor who had since become nationally known for his part in *Auf Wiedersehen Pet*. Afterwards he proudly recounted their conversation. Tim had told him, 'Your son will go far in the business.' That meant a lot to my dad.

We flew to Paris on honeymoon, which started disastrously when we went the wrong way and got trapped in some remote part of Charles de Gaulle airport. Ali had told me she could speak French, but discovered *'Je voudrai … out of the airport'* wasn't quite fluent enough to get help. We were there for hours before a guard finally guided us out of a well-hidden staff exit. Once we'd made our escape things looked up: ahead of us we had five days alone abroad. I tried not to worry too much about the audition that was scheduled for when I got back. It was for a new series called *Army Wives*.

CHAPTER EIGHT

The part was Dave Tucker, a working-class Geordie lad with a troubled past. The child of a broken marriage, Tucker was brought up by his grandmother and had been in trouble from the start, progressing from school clown to petty criminal. Beginning with a bit of car theft, he graduated to threatening a police officer with a snooker cue and obstructing the course of justice by eating his driving licence. Basically he was a bit of a lad, but a loveable one. At eighteen he had nowhere else to go but the army. From there it was over to me.

This was roughly all I knew as I travelled to London for the audition. I was there on the strength of *Casualty*. Casting agent Jane Arnell had

IN THE ARMY NOW

cast that series and when she was hired to cast *Army Wives* she put my name forward. As usual, the auditioning process was long and drawn out. Initially I read alone for the scriptwriters and director and guess what – at the end of the audition they weren't sure about me.

Three days later I read with Angie Clark, who was to play my wife, Donna. She was fantastic and I knew she would get the part. I just wasn't sure about myself. As we left, Jane said she'd contact me soon. I suppose I must have looked disappointed, because at the last minute she called me back to tell me the part was mine. I took the first train home to Newcastle to celebrate: first class.

Two days before filming began I found myself reading with sixteen actresses. The part of my wife had to be recast, because at the last minute Angie had been offered a television play and decided to go for it.

At this stage the relationship between Tucker and Paddy Garvey was a secondary consideration. The focus was to be on the women left at home and the scriptwriters were working on the assumption that it was the Tucker–Donna relationship that would drive the narrative. With this in mind I was asked which of the sixteen actresses I thought I could work with best.

As we progressed through the list I hoped for some sort of chemistry to help me make a decision, but I had to wait until the very last audition to find it. The actress was from the north-east and there was a warmth about her as well as a sense of strength and independence that made you believe she could survive on her own. Director Zelda Baron and I agreed. There was no competition: Rosie Rowell it was.

The day before we started filming, I met the two other actors with whom I would work most closely, Jerome Flynn and Gary Love. Jerome and I had crossed paths once before at the Live Theatre, when he was working for the RSC, but only to say hello. There was certainly nothing to indicate that I'd be making my début on *Top of the Pops* with him in the near future. The three of us were sent on a training course together at Lichfield Barracks, just outside Birmingham. The idea was to get a feel for the military by spending the day following an assault course, but it was all a bit farcical. I jumped a wall, Jerome swung on a rope, Gary sat and watched, then we all went to the pub.

I wasn't really interested in the action aspect and I don't think the other two were either. My dad's father had fought in both wars, the first time at only fifteen, and my auntie had kept the letters he sent home, written in desperate circumstances when he thought he might have only days to live. They had made a big impression on me. As a foot soldier my grandad was shot more than once and saw many of his friends die a miserable death in the trenches. As a result he always impressed on me the grim reality of war and I had reservations about glamorizing it in any way with exciting action sequences. Instead, I hoped that the characters and their relationships would become the focus. Fortunately for me, that's the way the series went from the start.

The first six months of filming were spent in Birmingham. The whole cast and crew were stuck in the Holiday Inn together, which gave us a chance to get to know each other. Jerome, Gary and I got on well from the off. With Jerome there's simply nothing not to like. And although Gary's a Londoner, we come from similar backgrounds and have a lot in common – not least football (although, sadly, he's a Chelsea fan). While Jerome was as laid-back as it's possible to be, Gary had endless energy. I was instantly taken by his perpetual optimism and the way he managed to motivate everyone else on the show.

We knew from the beginning that the writing was good. What we hadn't bargained for was the immediate on- and off-screen chemistry between the three of us as Paddy Garvey, Dave Tucker and Tony Wilton. It's something money can't buy and casting directors can't anticipate, but when it works it's priceless.

As we worked our way through the early episodes it quickly became clear that the male characters were becoming progressively stronger as their relationship developed. As the focus changed, so did the title: *Army Wives* became *Soldier Soldier*.

My relationship with Jerome worked particularly well and it showed. We're very different people, from different backgrounds and with different

approaches to life, but maybe because of these differences we bounced off each other easily. In many ways he is the opposite of me. He's peaceful, easy to be around and, unusually for an entertainer, doesn't have an ego. In fact, there's something about him that's quite vulnerable. He could never harm anybody. Romy is also dead honest and that alone had a huge impact on our on-screen relationship. Because I trusted him completely I could relax and take risks I would never have taken otherwise.

The series was new and everyone was feeling their way along but at the same time we felt it was going well. Because the Tucker–Garvey relationship was developing fast we were given a lot of freedom to develop our characters and make changes when things didn't feel right. We would often speak to real soldiers at Lichfield, who would glance at the scripts and say, 'Nah. No one

would ever say this and that would *never* happen.' We'd pick up on these things and take them back to the executive producer, Chris Kelly, who was always great about it. He knew we were getting it from the horse's mouth, so we had some leeway to make changes. Gary in particular was very committed and would sometimes rewrite scenes. He also kept an eye on me, pulling me up if he thought I was cruising through a scene without thinking it through.

The first series went out in the autumn of 1991. It had originally been scheduled for the beginning of the year but when Saddam Hussein declared war on Kuwait, Chris Kelly decided it might be better to postpone screening until the situation

ON THE SET OF *SOLDIER, SOLDIER* **IN MÜNSTER. LEANING FORWARD BETWEEN ME AND JEROME IS GARY LOVE.**

settled down. Despite our optimism, the all-important viewing figures for the first series weren't good. Even my dad didn't like it at first, and he told me so.

We were only on a seven-episode contract and began to think we wouldn't get another go, but, in keeping with their philosophy, ITV persevered. The executives had confidence that in time people would become addicted to the relationships at the core of the series, and instead of giving up they asked themselves what they could do to make it work. In fact, *Soldier Soldier* would begin to pick up by episodes five and six, but, not knowing that at the time, they cast around for solutions. The answer they came up with was to set it against a foreign backdrop.

When I got the phone call asking if I'd do another series I wasn't sure. The public didn't like it. The press didn't like it. Nobody seemed to like it, and I was ready to pack it in. But when my agent called to say the second series was to be set in Hong Kong, it was time for a rethink. It took seconds to make up my mind, but it was going to mean a long time away and I had to break the news to Ali first.

'Ali, they're talking about eleven weeks in Hong Kong.'

'Shit.'

'And it's three and a half grand an episode.'

Silence.

'You'll have to come over, Ali,' I added quickly.

'Too bloody right.'

It was decided: I was off to Hong Kong and Ali would visit. We were the luckiest soldiers in the world and it was to continue that way, from Hong Kong to Cyprus and from there to New Zealand, Australia and finally South Africa. I'd done a bit of travelling by then, but being paid to spend a few months in South-East Asia was something else. And if that was the situation, I was going to make the most of it.

Before the fun started, I returned to the stage, appearing in *And a Nightingale Sang* with the Northern Stage Company followed by a short run as Jesus in the York Mystery Plays at York's Theatre Royal. The first was a pleasure, the second a disaster. It was only a one-month run and sold out before it started, so it seemed like a good idea at the time. What I didn't realize was that I was going to be one of only two professional actors in it.

The first night was organized chaos. Everyone was suffering from such terrible stage fright they were queuing up to be sick. We were down to ten disciples, the other two were off sick and there were two hundred and fifty terror-struck extras waiting in the wings with palm leaves for the entry into Jerusalem. They didn't have much to do: their lines were simply 'Hail, hail, hail. Blessed is the King of Israel', after which I would make my entrance on a donkey. 'Hail, hail, hail' went quite well but, overwhelmed by nerves, they completely lost it on the second line, lapsing into awkward silence. My big entrance was a complete non-event and pretty much set the tone for the rest of the show. They were so nervous they couldn't find the tables, chairs, bread or wine, and when I came out for the last supper there was nothing there. They all looked at me expecting a miracle.

Added to all that, it was a five-hour show, with the curtain coming down at one in the morning, by which time the place was full of pensioners and schoolkids nodding off in the stalls. The night Ali brought the in-laws a woman had a heart attack in the dress circle as I was being nailed to the cross. It was that kind of production.

We got very mixed reviews. The *Independent* was especially damning: 'I do not know what Robson Green was playing at but it was hard to believe anyone would follow him across the stage let alone Israel.' The local papers agreed, but the *Mail* and the *Guardian* heaped praise on it. Personally, I got a lot of flak from the Christian contingent. I tried to play Jesus as a normal bloke faced with a terrible dilemma, but people didn't want a vulnerable bloke in a T-shirt and jeans. They wanted the all-knowing Jesus in white, flowing robes, long hair and a beard. At least it was a hit with one person in the audience. My mam loved it.

It was a relief to get away for the second series of *Soldier Soldier*, although the change of scenery was a shock to my system. They say you can see people hanging out their washing when you come in to land in Hong Kong and it's true. The city engulfs you from the moment you touch down and it's an incredible visual experience: the mish-mash

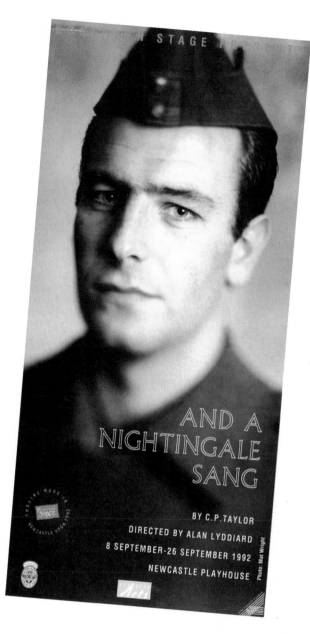

AND A
NIGHTINGALE
SANG

BY C.P. TAYLOR
DIRECTED BY ALAN LYDDIARD
8 SEPTEMBER-26 SEPTEMBER 1992
NEWCASTLE PLAYHOUSE

LEFT: BACK IN UNIFORM FOR *AND A NIGHTINGALE SANG,* **FOR THE NORTHERN STAGE COMPANY, NEWCASTLE. ABOVE, FROM LEFT: VAL MCLANE, ME , DAVID WHITTAKER AND DENISE WELCH.**

GETTING AN EARFUL FROM ROBERT SPENDLOVE DURING THE FILMING OF *SOLDIER SOLDIER* **IN MÜNSTER.**

of ultra-modern architecture and shanty town, the pollution, the traffic, the frantic pace of life. It's almost too much to take in.

Someone smarter than me must have anticipated the combined effects of culture shock and jet lag, because we were given eight days to recover and adjust before filming started. My initial reaction was: 'Bugger jet lag. I'm fine, I'm here, I'm being paid a fortune and it's hot.' Within an hour I had collapsed at the hotel, in a bed the size of a football pitch.

It was a great week and we were treated like royalty. Our tour started with a boat trip to Causeway Bay Harbour. We filled the boat – me, Jerome, Gary, Jim Carter, Miles Anderson, Holly Aird, Rosie Rowell, Sara Garner, Chris Kelly, Annie Tricklebank and everyone else on the production – just standing on the deck, floating across the bay as the sun hovered on the horizon.

I was having the time of my life. Away from the hysteria of the city, we visited beautiful islands off the coast, lazed around in idyllic lagoons and lived on fresh seafood. Even Jim Carter, who was the most experienced among us, said, 'You've got to treasure these moments, man. We're just in this incredible situation and it doesn't happen often.' By the time we were ready to start filming the mood was just right. Everyone was very relaxed and the company felt like a unit.

Hong Kong also had its seedier side and Chris Kelly found himself negotiating with the Triads for permission to film in the heart of the city. It was an edgy business and with the Triads so well established on the island we knew we couldn't turn to the police for help if things got out of hand. Fortunately, a combination of grovelling and hard cash got us what we wanted. Only slightly less terrifying were the Welsh Guards – all six foot plus, hard as nails and not keen on actors. We filmed with them for most of our time there and they gave us a lot of stick. They were pursuing a tough career which involved very real risks and there we were, a crew of poncey actors whose biggest worries were lines and make-up. I wasn't about to argue.

We knew as soon as we started on the second series that something was going to happen. Dramatically, it worked well to introduce a group of English squaddies to a foreign culture, and I was very happy with the way Tucker was working out. It was a challenge to try to break down some of the stereotypes usually applied to a man like him. On the surface he fitted the general perception of a squaddie, but we wanted to show that things are never that simple. The same applied to the wives. Instead of portraying them as strong women, stoically coping while the men are away,

ENJOYING SOME R AND R WITH MAM IN HONG KONG DURING THE PRODUCTION OF *SOLDIER SOLDIER.*

TRYING TO KEEP UP WITH PAULETTE IVORY (SECOND FROM LEFT) IN A DANCE SEQUENCE FROM *PIAF*.

we went for a much more realistic take on what happens when couples are separated for long periods of time. Unlike the *Top Gun* version of military life, the series tried hard to be honest. In time we started dealing with suicide in the forces and issues like racism and homophobia. It suited me down to the ground: real, character-driven situations, good scripts and not too many tanks and gun battles.

The only drawback was being so far from Ali. It was an eleven-week stint, which is a long time apart, especially for the one who's not going anywhere. We knew it would be difficult, but I was surprised by how much I missed her and although she had a heavy case-load at the time I managed to persuade her to come out for a visit and bring my mam with her. 'Eee, she's been missing you,' were Mam's first words. I kept my thoughts to myself. It had been six weeks since

we'd seen each other and I was just about ready to rip her clothes off.

Everyone was brilliant and really looked after my mam. She took to it like a duck to water. On the first evening she rang me from her room to say: 'That complimentary tea set they give you is absolutely marvellous, isn't it? It'll make a lovely present.'

'Which complimentary tea set is that then, Mam?'

'The waiter brought it in. "Compliments of the hotel," he said.'

'That's the *tea*, Mam,' I tried to explain. By that time she already had it wrapped, bagged and ready for shipping back to England.

As we had hoped, the second series took off like a rocket, doubling in popularity within weeks. The press picked up on it and we got a lot of good feedback from the public, particularly soldiers and would-be soldiers. Completely by accident, it turned out to be a great PR machine for the army.

Word got back to us that young guys were turning up in droves to enlist, asking to join 'that unit where they go all over the place and have a brilliant time', apparently oblivious to the fact that the regiment was a figment of Chris Kelly's imagination.

There was no problem with getting the green light for another series. The call came through after the second episode of the second series was broadcast and this time I didn't hesitate. There were rumours that we might be going to New Zealand, and I knew the series had potential in terms of where it could lead my career.

Initially, *Soldier Soldier* hadn't had much impact on my life outside work. The shouts just changed from 'Oi, Jimmy' to 'Oi, Tucker'. But as the viewing figures rose I was recognized everywhere, especially in Newcastle. Press interest was growing too. Where there had once been a handful of reporters wanting to ask questions, there was suddenly a packed room. Inevitably the questioning became more intrusive, moving from 'What does your wife do and when did you meet?' to 'Who are your ex-girlfriends?' and 'When are you and wife going to start a family?' I once mentioned a crush on my music teacher and she ended up with the press at the door, despite the fact that I was only five when we knew each other. I learned to be more cautious.

Behind a lot of the questions about my personal life was the assumption that for Ali it was excluding or even threatening to be outside the industry. It may have been a problem for the press, but it was never a problem for us. There are some husbands and wives who hang around the set, worrying about what would be going on if they didn't, but they are rare. The truth is that there's no worse place to be if you're not actively involved. Actors spend half of their time repeating the smallest of scenes again and again and the other half waiting around to be called. For the actor, with a vision of how the whole picture fits together, that's fine, but for anyone else the novelty of life on set wears off fast. Ali was

IN *PIAF* WITH SINGER AND ACTRESS MARILYN CUTTS.

never as interested in the acting anyway; she was always more interested in the technical side: how continuity works, make-up, direction. She always had her own career and although we missed each other, we both had our own lives to get on with.

In 1988 I had a few months' break and took on a three-week run in *Piaf* at the Tyne Theatre. I was what is called 'players cast', which means I played whatever was needed – onion seller, passer-by, Piaf's agent and the boxer she marries. I had fancied it because it was a chance to do music hall and it's a great story, but it was panned. I knew I was in trouble when the director started asking me to 'heighten'.

'Heighten?' I repeated, confused.

'Yes, when you act you must heighten.'

'What do you mean, "heighten"?'

'As you speak your lines, heighten; heighten from the heart.'

I didn't have a clue what he was on about. Maybe that's why it was panned: nobody knew how to heighten.

I came out of *Piaf* with bad crits but a new agent. Like many actors, I have an ambivalent attitude towards agents and had managed without one since leaving Dave Holley during *Casualty*. I felt I'd outgrown him, but it had been a hard decision to make. He'd done a good job early on and was the only one who stood up and fought for me when I was trying to get my Equity card. It was before the Live Theatre came along and although I wasn't on the verge of going professional at that stage I desperately wanted the card and tried to get it on the basis of my singing with the Worky Tickets. There were only two cards and four hopefuls. I was up against a stripper – an 'exotic dancer' as they were known – a dancer and a magician; we were all considered variety acts.

Dave Holley was fighting my corner, but the man with the final say was a guy called Harry Higgins, the chairman of the Gateshead branch and a well-known character actor in Newcastle. He gave the cards to the stripper and the dancer, saying that I didn't have enough experience. I'd been acting and singing for years by then, and I disagreed with his decision. Years later I was asked to get involved in a video called *Tucker's*

Story, set fifty years in the future. I wanted nothing to do with it. So who did they find to play Tucker as an old man reflecting on his life? Harry Higgins.

I was in no hurry to get another agent, because I was getting work through people who had seen me in other things, but when an opportunity came along and the director of *Piaf* recommended his agent, I went with it. It was a short relationship which came to a sticky end over an advert and did nothing to restore my faith in agents.

I was already in *Soldier Soldier* when she and I met, so there was no real pressure to find me work. Nevertheless, she was keen to earn her keep and when I received a message to call her urgently I was curious to hear what she had come up with. 'Robson, I've got some great news,' she started excitedly. 'I've got you a fantastic deal on a Toffee Crisp advert.'

She talked it up wildly, reeling off the director's previous achievements in great detail as if it was a Hollywood movie we were discussing. There was a long pause.

'Uh, hold on a minute. We're talking about a toffee bar here. I'm not interested.' This clearly wasn't the response she was expecting.

'Robson, I think you're going to have to get down off your high horse… ' she began.

'I beg your pardon,' I interrupted.

'…and this northern lad image. I've been meaning to talk to you about it. It means you can only be put up for certain parts, which is very restricting.'

Coming from someone who had already made a fortune from my 'northern lad image', this was a bit rich, and I couldn't help but point it out. 'Listen,' I began, feeling my temper rising, 'I think there's something important here that you've missed. I *am* a lad from the north. Firstly, I'm in no hurry to cover it up, and on top of that, I don't see why being from the north should be limiting.'

But she wasn't deterred and continued to press me, adding that I should really move to London if I wanted to work. At this point I'd heard enough.

'First you take fifteen per cent from me every week for work I found myself and then you have the audacity to insult who I am and where I come from.'

I put the phone down and faxed her to say that I was no longer her client. I could afford to relax. I had New Zealand to look forward to.

CHAPTER NINE

After the madness of Hong Kong, New Zealand couldn't have been more different. Jerome and I fell in love with the place. Where the exotic Hong Kong landscape changes before your eyes, rural New Zealand seemed untouched by time. The hairs prickled on the back of my neck as we were greeted with a *haka*, the traditional Maori war dance. It had a sense of history, drama and spirituality perfectly matched to the surroundings and set the tone for the weeks to come.

We were based in the middle of the North Island, at a small army camp in Waiouru which bordered Maori land. The local pub was more like a house that sold beer and that's where we converged to relax over

UNCHAINED MELODY

a few pints of Black Gold. The owner thought all his Christmases had come at once and probably earned enough to retire on before we left.

With four weeks of filming ahead of us we were given a few days to acclimatize and on the second day Jerome, Gary, Dorian Healey and I decided to head into Alkuni, the nearest town, and organize a trip. On a whim we decided to try white-water rafting. Actors on the verge of filming are not allowed to play football, never mind white-water rafting, so from the beginning there was a mild feeling of conspiracy and adventure. This turned to high anxiety as we drove out to a mountainous northern region, past cascading rivers and rocky waterfalls to meet our instructors.

The two Kiwi guides gave us a two-minute crash course in white-water rafting. They seemed to know what they were doing and were full of laugh-a-minute stories of previous disasters: the guy who broke both arms; the time another guy was under for five minutes before they got him out and brought him round. We assumed this was a regular spiel aimed at frightening townies like us, although at the same time I couldn't help noticing that no one was laughing. Jerome and Gary seemed cool enough, but Dorian and I had gone very quiet. We listened carefully as the Kiwis talked us through things.

'This is a grade-five river, OK?'

'Right. So where does five actually come in the scale then?'

'The scale stops at five.'

'Right.'

'When we get to the waterfall, you hold on.'

'What waterfall?'

'Then I'll shout, "Paddle left" and you'll all need to lean and paddle. If anyone falls out, nobody jump in.'

I knew as soon as I stepped into the raft that it was all a terrible mistake, but by now the situation had gathered its own momentum. Within minutes of setting off, one of the guys warned us that the waterfall was coming up. There was a shout of 'Hold on', followed by a chorus of 'Oh fuck' from the rest of us. One minute we were bumping and crashing along and the next the horizon just disappeared. Instead of sliding over the edge as it should have, the boat seemed to stop dead for a moment, then dived at ninety degrees. I had been holding on obediently up to that point, but faced with the twenty-foot drop ahead I panicked and, at the crucial moment, I let go and yelled.

The next thing I knew I was under the waterfall, crashing downwards and gasping for air. It happened too fast to feel fear and my first thought was, so this is it – this is drowning. I'd hoped for something fast and painless and this was how I was going to go. Everything was pitch-black. All my energy had gone on struggling against the water and there was no oxygen left to even hold my breath. Suddenly I surfaced and felt something solid above me. I was under the boat in an air pocket. Holding on obviously hadn't done much to help the others either: they were all in the water and clinging to the upturned boat.

I didn't know where I was. I could hear them somewhere nearby shouting my name, but I couldn't speak — not in any kind of intelligible way anyway. I was crying my eyes out, the boat was still moving and for all I knew there could have been another waterfall on the way. After what seemed like hours one of the others managed to yank me out. Gary was grabbing me and shouting, 'Where the fuck have you been? We thought you were dead.' I was too busy trying to get my hands on the instructor to answer.

Back on shore we gave the guys a hard time. The bravado had gone and it was clear they had been as terrified as we were. We drove the two hours back to the hotel in silence. Nobody said a word.

As expected, we got a bollocking when we arrived back. The only one who didn't seem too bothered was Ali. When I phoned home with the story, by now honed and ready for dining out on, she just told me how stupid I was. I was always saying, 'You don't know how close you came to losing me today', so I think she'd already heard one too many dramatic near-death stories to recognize a real one.

Ali and I spoke on the phone three or four times a day, even if it was just for a few minutes. I know people thought it was strange, particularly in New Zealand, when I also wrote every day and Ali wrote back. When people spotted the pile of letters on the desk in my room I could see that they were wondering what on earth we found to say to each

other. I would just write about what I saw around me, send pictures and try to share the experience with her.

As an actor you drop into other cultures and lives for a very short stay, but sometimes you take something quite profound away with you. This was definitely the case in rural New Zealand and that moment for me came on the first day of filming. The scene had us digging trenches down in a beautiful valley near Waiouru and we were waiting for someone to call 'Action' when we heard a strange thundering noise gradually growing louder. We were beginning to think it was an earthquake when suddenly hundreds and hundreds of wild horses appeared on the horizon at the entrance to the valley. On spotting us they all ground to a nervous halt, except for one stallion, who stepped forward to see what we were up to on their patch. Satisfied, he turned on his heels and led the others back out of the valley.

It was an unexpected moment and a reminder of how far we were from the cashpoint culture of home and the humdrum of nine-to-five city life.

Sadly, only three episodes were shot in New Zealand. After that we returned to Münster, West Germany, where we were based in a real army barracks. For the next four months we were the guests of the 1st Battalion of the Coldstream Guards, who were all Geordies. We were sharing their barracks and initially there were general expectations that I lived the life of Tucker off screen. Shortly after arriving we were invited to a disco so that the actors and soldiers could get to know each other. There was a free bar with unlimited supplies; it was a recipe for disaster. By three in the morning Jerome, Gary and I found ourselves propping up the bar while the soldiers cycled round the dance floor on bikes to Sade's *Smooth Operator*. Even Tucker couldn't have kept up with these guys.

While we were there the troops were either returning from or preparing to go to Bosnia. That was strange: they were fighting a real war, whereas once again the feeling of being actors pretending to be soldiers – and being paid a fortune for it – was something of which we were very conscious. On one occasion four busloads of soldiers arrived back from Bosnia as we were filming a sequence in the parade ground. Their wives and families were there waiting for them, but the third assistant director, worried that his scene was going to be ruined, demanded that the buses be stopped from crossing the parade ground to the waiting families. It was insensitive to the point of madness. Within minutes a Geordie soldier built like a brick shithouse had him up against a wall while the others walked straight through the film crew and cameras to their wives.

In general I wasn't entirely comfortable in Germany. I found it a deeply conservative country and sometimes felt that there was an underlying racism that had never quite gone away. The

HARD AT WORK IN CYPRUS. WITH HIS BACK TO THE CAMERA IS DORIAN HEALY, WHILE GARY LOVE IS BEHIND JEROME AND I.

IN SOUTH AFRICA WITH
SOLDIER SOLDIER.

advantage of being there was being able to see more of Ali and my family. I missed them all and I missed Newcastle. When Dawn and my mam came over for a week I felt so homesick I was in tears when I met them at the airport. I flew home as often as I could and when I was there I would just rest.

Ali and I were still living in Tynemouth and when I was at home I relaxed by walking on the beach and catching up on all the telly I'd missed. Other friends were actors and most were working nights, so Ali and I led a pretty quiet life. I hadn't really kept in touch with people from school or the shipyard. Acting had made me an outsider at school and after that I never got into the pub culture of the north-east. On the rare occasions when I did bump into someone we usually found that we had little in common, although there were the odd exceptions. Steve Williamson was one of those and it was probably because we were both a bit different.

At school we called him 'the Professor' because he wore little round glasses and looked intelligent. I remember him moving to the area and starting at our school. On his first day we had biology and we were examining an onion skin under a microscope. When we were asked to identify the pattern made by the structure his was the only hand to shoot up. 'Tessellated hexagon,' he answered. Even the teacher was stunned. We were both oddballs and got friendly. I used to pay him to do my homework and he ended up playing bass with Solid State.

I bumped into Steve years later when he came to see me in a play I did between series of *Soldier Soldier* called *Your Home in the West*. It was lovely seeing him and we found we still had lots to talk about, but he was a rare exception.

I don't know why I persisted in being different as a kid and I don't remember considering the option of changing to fit in. I was the way I was and enjoyed performing so much that there was no other option, even if it alienated me from other lads. But it wasn't just the acting that set me apart.

Surrounded by women as a child, I identified with their expressiveness and sensitivity much more than with the macho alternative, which is very pronounced in the north-east. I was more interested in what girls and women talked about and the ease with which they did it. It was always much easier to talk with my mam and as I got older I found the same applied to other girls and women. The men and boys around me weren't any less emotional, but it was something they kept under wraps. I felt lucky. Through acting I found the perfect outlet for emotional expression. Some men find it in a football crowd; others never find it at all.

With *Soldier Soldier* still going from strength to strength, I started getting other offers for television work, but nothing that appealed to me. The offers were mostly for situation comedies and although I enjoyed comedy I always found it worked better for me when it sprang from real situations within a dramatic context. One-liners and canned laughter weren't my style. My instincts told me it was worth hanging on for the right TV role, and rather than take anything else I returned to theatre in the breaks between series.

When we were asked to do a fourth series, Gary and Jerome and I got together to talk money. Once it occurs to you that they need you as much as you need them, that changes the rules of the game. It's important to know your worth as an actor, particularly when the going is good, because you know it may not stay that way. We all read trade papers and realized what fourteen million viewers meant in terms of profit margins and advertising revenue. We also knew that if we stuck together we had bargaining power and we were right. The money went up and we stayed.

The next stop was sunny Cyprus; the combination of an exotic backdrop and culture clash was working so well it would have been stupid to change it. We had a look at the scripts. The story-lines were still strong and the first three scripts had us on R and R, Rest and Recuperation. Loosely translated, this means the boys mess around, drink a few beers and go swimming a lot. We had no complaints.

We were based in the beautiful little mountain village of Pissouri and our driver, Kypros, turned out to be *the* man to know. Not only did he run the only bar in the village, where his home-made wine kept the crew happy, but he was a mine of local information. As we got to know him he told us about the Turkish invasion of northern Cyprus in 1974, when his house was bombed by Phantoms and many of his relatives lost their lives. Although the main story lines were set, the producers were always willing to look for local context to drive the story along, and Kypros became a kind of informal political consultant and some of his stories were incorporated into the scripts.

By now we were so relaxed with one another and the characters that we were having a lot of fun with the series. It all

PERFORMING *YOUR HOME IN THE WEST* **AT THE LIVE THEATRE WITH MY GREAT FRIEND TREVOR FOX.**

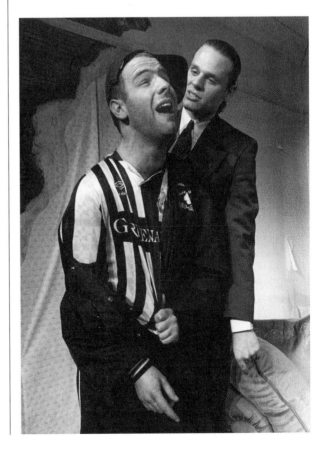

seemed a long way from those early days on *Casualty* when work was a constant battle with nerves. Now, in such a laid-back atmosphere, we were able to improvise and the on-screen results were great.

After six weeks in Cyprus we were whisked back to Münster for a few weeks, then on to England for the big wedding episode. The plot at that stage was that officers Kate Butler and Kieran Voce finally marry and the squaddies club together to hire a band for the wedding. When the band don't show, Tucker and Garvey have to take to the stage.

The suggestion that Tucker and Garvey could sing at the wedding had been put forward by Jerome and me at a production meeting weeks earlier. Both of us were notorious for singing on set and the idea of making an album together was a running joke, although it was very definitely a joke at that stage. When the wedding scene was being written it seemed the obvious solution: Jerome had inherited a great voice from his dad, the actor and singer Eric Flynn, while I had a background with the Worky Tickets, and most important, we both liked the same kind of music.

Initially we suggested an old Sam Cooke or Eddie Cochran number: a good, fast-moving, R&B classic which would allow the crowd to join in. It was the producer, Annie Tricklebank, who came back to us with *Unchained Melody*. I was dead against it.

'Annie, man, this is Tucker. There's no way he would sing something like *Unchained Melody*. It just doesn't gel.'

'But you're singing a song that reflects on your life. Trust me.'

I was adamant that it wasn't right, not to mention terrified of taking on such a complex, delicate, free-floating melody.

'No. Change the song. I don't like the song,' I insisted.

There was only one person who could have swayed me at this point. Calmly, Romy persuaded me to give it a go. The first time round, we murdered it, which left me convinced it was a bad idea, but somehow he managed to coax me into giving it just one more try, this time as part of the scene.

I told myself to play the honesty of it. The band don't show, the curtain rises and we sing. As we got off to a faltering start I realized why Annie had chosen *Unchained Melody*. It wasn't simply a lovely song: it tied in perfectly with Tucker's story-line, giving the scene real poignancy. As he sings – 'I need your love, I want your love. Please give your love to me' – his wife, Donna, is having an affair with another man. As the final notes faded out everyone on the set applauded. The reaction was immediate and the crew even joked that it was a potential number one. They loved it. Annie loved it. Everyone loved it. I was outnumbered.

The episode was screened in October 1994 and the following day there was pandemonium. The reaction was enormous. We had an audience of over sixteen million at the time and it seemed like a fair proportion had stormed their local record shop the next morning and demanded to buy a record that didn't exist: *Unchained Melody* by Robson Green and Jerome Flynn.

It wasn't long before we were tracked down by Simon Cowell, A&R man for RCA. Where there was a demand he was keen to meet it. Initially we were about as keen on making the record as we had been about doing the song in the first place, but Simon wasn't the kind of guy to give up easily. He rang my agent and the director almost daily and even took to phoning my mam, thinking she would be able to persuade me.

On one side, Mam and my agent were in favour. On the other, Ali, Sandra and I were dead against it. My main problem with the idea was that I was an actor and that's where I wanted to channel my energies. I was also aware that actors-turned-pop stars risked serious credibility problems. On top of that, I felt distanced from chart music. There had been a time when rushing out for a new single and religiously watching *Top of the Pops* were highlights of the week. I'd even been a DJ for a while. But now, in 1994, at a time when rave and techno dominated the music scene, I felt completely removed from it all.

As we continued to fight off Simon Cowell's offers, both Jerome and I were also being pressed to sign up for our fifth series of *Soldier Soldier*. Neither of had ever intended to stay with the series this long, but the camaraderie and the

opportunity to travel had kept us coming back for more. The final carrot was Australia, followed by South Africa. Jerome decided to do half the series and bow out after Australia. I signed up for the full series but let them know it would be my last.

We were still enjoying it, although we both knew it was time to move on. The series had been running so long around the same domestic relationships, it was in danger of becoming a soap. Now there's nothing wrong with a good soap – there have been classic episodes of *Coronation Street* that could stand up as mini-dramas in themselves – but I was in danger of becoming typecast as the loveable rogue, and knew that it was time for a change.

Usually pay negotiations take weeks, but by the last series we did (there would be another two without us) they took hours. We told them what we wanted and they said yes. With *Soldier Soldier* we had reached a huge audience, which peaked at over sixteen million. It was at that point that actors start to feel their power and I was no exception. It wasn't the power in itself that was appealing but the freedom that came with success, the realization that I could start to do the things I really wanted to do.

One of my long-term aims was to get my own production company off the ground and *Soldier Soldier* had provided me with the profile and the finance I needed to get started. I was very interested in the idea of building up a company in the north-east. It was a way of reinvesting in the area I came from and providing opportunities for local writers and actors. I knew there was so much talent in Newcastle but few outlets for it and almost no means of taking it to a wider audience. There is a strong feeling in Newcastle that London turns its back on the north, but I wanted to do whatever I could to change that.

We'd already tried our hand at a few pop videos for local artists during the fourth series of *Soldier Soldier*, operating under the name Citizen Films. Our next goal was television. I knew early on that in order to set up premises, hire staff and buy scripts to take to the networks, we would need a huge amount of capital. Even if it did well the company would probably run at a loss for a few years, but I hoped that the fees I could now command as an actor would keep the company afloat.

The original directors were Andrew Gunn, a focus puller, and Ian Cottage, an animator, both friends I had met years earlier through the theatre. After seeing me in *The Long Line*, Andrew had cast me in a short he had made at film school called *In Search of Perfection and Mermaids*, in which I played a down-and-out who falls in love with a mermaid and ends up following her into the sea. We'd remained friends since and set up the company together.

With a television project in mind, Gary Love, by now a close friend, came on board and together we set about making *Come Snow, Come Blow*. We had started the pre-production during series four of *Soldier Soldier* and planned to continue with filming before and during series five. It was a heavy workload which would involve keeping several balls in the air at once, another reason I was loath to get involved with making a single.

Come Snow, Come Blow was written by Leonard Barras, Newcastle's finest surrealist writer. Along with Tom Hadaway, Barras had been one of the original members of the Society of Northern Writers, but twenty-five years later he was still little known outside the north. The play revolves around Ivan and Atwood Ruddy, a pair of bachelor brothers who share a little council flat. Atwood is training for the Olympics but he's fourteen stone and his only experience is the Morpeth to Newcastle road race, from which he was disqualified for catching the bus. Ivan works for a plastic moulding factory and the two live in a constant state of misunderstanding.

I had loved the play since performing in it at the Live Theatre and really wanted to bring it to the screen. Tim Healy and Donald McBride were cast as Atwood (the part I had played on stage) and Ivan, with Rodney Bewes as the gas man, whose mission in life is to read their meter. The budget was very tight and no one was in it to make their fortune. As is often the case when people are starting out and are strapped for cash, there was a great feeling of optimism, and everyone pulled together to make it work. We were using a lot of people from the *Soldier Soldier* crew who were prepared to take a cut in wages to be involved. My brother, David, helped out, my mam made sandwiches and friends pitched in wherever they

could. We even had help from local businesses: Jim Kerr, a local brewery owner interested in putting something back into the community, let us use the brewery as the set for the factory and provided location food.

Gary Love directed, for the first time but brilliantly. He's a great motivator and I knew from our days together on *Soldier Soldier* that he could take it on. I was never tempted to direct. It's a huge job which takes in everything from realizing the overall vision to making sure the crew get their lunch on time and motivating actors found crying in their trailer. A big part of it for me was winning the confidence of the writers in the area who had been neglected for so long and were now understandably cautious about some young guy steaming in with a camera crew.

Come Snow, Come Blow was conceived as a half-hour pilot for a six-parter, but we didn't have a commission, which meant we were making the programme on spec with no guarantee that a network TV channel would take it up. Philip Rays from Carlton had expressed interest in the script and helped with cars, contacts, distribution and securing permissions to film, but without a commission we were definitely taking a gamble. What kept us going was confidence in the script. I wanted a lot of people to see Lenny's work.

Christmas was fast approaching and, despite constant requests from record retailers for the single, Simon was forced to abandon plans for a Christmas number one – for that year at least. Jerome was planning to head off after Christmas for some R and R in India and Nepal and my mind was on developments at Coastal Productions, as we were now called.

It was a good time to tie up loose ends, so I called Simon Cowell at RCA's Fulham office to confirm conclusively that we would not be making the record. I wasn't prepared for his response and when he mentioned the advance RCA had in mind it took my breath away. As the Yanks say, money

talks and bullshit walks. I was definitely weakening and, after a second discussion, I finally agreed. There was just one condition: I was only up for it if Jerome was too.

AS ATWOOD RUDDY, WITH DENISE BRYSON, IN *COME SNOW, COME BLOW*.

Jerome had initially been willing to meet Simon, but I had talked him out of the whole idea. Now that he'd taken himself off to the other side of the world to relax and meditate, I was ringing him with a change of heart. I had no idea what his reaction might be. The village where he was staying may have been remote, but it had a fax and I sent a brief message: 'Jerome. Phone me urgently. Need to speak to you.'

He rang straight back.

'But I thought you weren't interested,' he protested when I told him I was reconsidering the whole idea.

'Well … they are offering a lot of money.'

'How much?'

'Twenty-five grand.'

'What!'

'Each.'

There was a long silence, but it told me exactly what I needed to know. It was silly money for a few days in a studio and we knew we'd be crazy to turn it down.

WITH THE CAST OF *COME SNOW, COME BLOW*. BACK ROW FROM LEFT: TIM HEALY, ME, DIRECTOR GARY LOVE. FRONT ROW: DONALD MCBRIDE, DENISE WELCH AND RODNEY BEWES.

The first thing we did was get a good lawyer. I knew nothing about the music business and the little I'd picked up through a friendship with Brian Hibbard of the Flying Pickets wasn't encouraging. It's a ruthless world and we just wanted to make a flying visit and get out in one piece. We were put in touch with John Kennedy, who had worked on Band Aid. He was expensive but fantastic; his advice was to treat the record as a one-off novelty single and sign a short six-month contract. The standard music contract is closer to five years, over which time the royalties are fixed, which is why so many young artists get stitched up when go from nowhere to *Top of the Pops* in a few years. It was good advice, but at the time we

didn't realize how good. With the deal set up and recording dates pencilled in, we flew to Australia to film our fifth and final series of *Soldier Soldier*.

Now that we had made the decision to quit, the last series was a ball. We were fearless and it was flying off the page. Australia provided the most dramatic of backdrops so far. There was a real sense of the place as a primitive land, with the Aborigines the clearest reminder of the country's past. When we filmed it was with their OK or not at all. If they approved, they blessed the land where we were filming, but if it was sacred land we respected the fact and steered clear. Happy with the arrangement, the elders would sometimes come and sit on set and just watch in silence.

We also visited villages where Aborigines were reclaiming their land and history and met an great Australian actor called Michael, who was working to re-educate Aborigines from whom everything had been stolen. The way Michael explained it was: 'They've been sleeping and dreaming for 40,000 years and they've been having nightmares for the last hundred.' He lent me a book, *Taken by the White Man*, which described the way the Aboriginal culture had been destroyed in the most brutal of ways. I was staggered to read that it was only in the 1960s that permits were withheld for shooting Aborigines. At the same time, when Michael talked about Aboriginal concepts like walkabout and astrotravel, there was a feeling that these people were years ahead of us.

It was the last stop for Jerome. Without him I knew the series would lose an essential ingredient: it would lose its spirit. Our final scenes together had an energy of their own and as we said our goodbyes we knew we could have done it without a script and that there was no acting required.

On our own small scale it felt like the end of an era.

CHAPTER TEN

I came back to mayhem: from the moment the plane touched down it was all systems go. The next year was to be one of the busiest of my life and it included its disappointments as well as triumphs. The first disappointment was the reaction to *Come Snow, Come Blow*. I'd been working on it throughout the last series of *Soldier Soldier* and we had been pleased with the end result, but the network took one look and shook their heads. It was too surreal; the people making the decisions just couldn't work out what it was about or how to pigeon-hole it. For everyone involved it was a huge disappointment.

It's very hard to anticipate how far you can go when your aim is to succeed in mainstream television. We knew the idea was anarchic and

FACING THE MUSIC

offbeat, but there was also a strong underlying reality and I thought we'd got the balance right. One of the most encouraging things was that the crew had laughed themselves silly all the way through filming and they were usually a good gauge of public opinion. But Leonard Barras is an acquired taste and maybe the expectation of television is that it must work right away or you've lost your audience.

It was a difficult time. A lot of the people involved were friends as well as professional colleagues and it was hard when they kept ringing up and asking, 'When's it going on?' In the end we had to accept that as it stood, it wasn't going on

AS RORY CONNOR IN *THE GAMBLING MAN*, FOR TYNE TEES TELEVISION.

at all, and we decided to put it on the back burner and come back and rework it when we could.

Although our involvement with the music business had begun so half-heartedly, it was now paying off at a time when I needed to recover from the failure of *Come Snow, Come Blow*. We had flown back and cut the single between episodes in Australia at the Southwark studios of the legendary producers Mike Stock and Matt Aitken. Simon made them his first choice, saying they had 'golden ears for a pop opportunity' and with thirteen number-one singles to their credit we figured they knew what they were doing. For the flip side of the single Simon had settled on *The White Cliffs Of Dover* and wanted to release it as a double A-side on 8 May 1995, the fiftieth anniversary of VE Day.

We still had mixed feelings about the whole thing. It was a year since the episode featuring *Unchained Melody* had gone out and we weren't convinced that the interest would still be there. By now we had put a fair bit of time into the project. In addition to the single, there had to be a promotional video, for which I suggested Norman Stone as director.

Norman and I had worked together on *The Gambling Man* a few years earlier and it had just been screened. It was a three-part drama adapted from a Catherine Cookson novel and it was classic Cookson: the poor people have black teeth and lots of muck on their faces and fall in love with the poshies. As Mike Elliot, a comedian well known in Newcastle, says, 'In literature there are only five stories and everything else is a variation on those five – Catherine Cookson should master the other four.' For me it was my version of *The Cincinnati Kid*, a favourite Steve McQueen movie. I got to play the hero and die saving my club-footed brother from a fire at the end. It was never going to win me a BAFTA but my mam loved it and it was a lot of fun to make.

I knew Norman could make the video standing on his head. We worked well together and he had a background in drama and music video, having directed Pink Floyd, Cliff Richard and Duran

Duran. With actors rather than singers at his disposal, he came up with video that told a story. *Unchained Melody* was intercut with scenes from the black and white romantic classic *Brief Encounter* and *The White Cliffs Of Dover* became the soundtrack to a series of historical blows for freedom: the declaration of peace at the end of the Second World War, the homecoming of Terry Waite, the fall of the Berlin Wall and the release of Nelson Mandela.

RCA were handling the release very carefully. There were to be no sneak previews before the official release date – with one exception: we were to appear live on Cilla Black's *Surprise, Surprise* in front of an audience of fourteen million.

When the moment arrived to step from the wings I was way beyond terrified. Cilla Black was an icon. All I could hear was a staccato *Step Inside Love* going through my head. Singing on live TV was something I had never imagined myself doing and without the extremely calming influence of Jerome at my side I don't think I could have done it. As it turned out, this was only the first of many nerve-racking performances.

When the single was released there were already advance orders of 150,000 in record shops up and down the country, and at the close of business on the first day repeat orders topped 300,000. It was clear we had a monster on our hands and Simon wasn't the least bit surprised when *Unchained Melody* became one of the fastest-selling pop singles in history by the end of the first week.

If we were unprepared for the single's success, we were equally taken aback by the response of the music press. They hated us, they hated the single and Radio One refused to play it – until, that is, they were left with no choice. Despite getting next to no airplay, *Unchained Melody* slid past Oasis, Pulp and Take That and was number one within six days of its release, making it the fastest-selling single of the nineties. It was a bloody miracle.

By accident rather than design, we ended up with one of the best record deals in history. Things moved so fast that the record was on sale before we had signed anything beyond the initial contract. Naturally, with the single doing so well there was talk of an album and we were suddenly in a very strong position. It was like a runaway train. While we were pondering the legal situation, over two million people bought the single and our initial reluctance to pursue our advantage, which had actually been brought about by lack of confidence, was interpreted as cannily holding out for more. We asked John Kennedy what we stood to make if we went ahead with the album deal. 'Oh,' he said casually, 'you'll be millionaires.' It was like a fairy-tale. When the album, *Robson and Jerome*, was released, he was proved right: it stayed at number one in the album charts for seven weeks, just as the single had. We had been pushed and shoved every inch of the way and now they were talking in seven figures.

Live appearances didn't get any easier. After Cilla came a couple of Royal Variety Performances (I took my mam and Auntie Pat, who were both more excited about catching a glimpse of Lionel Richie and Cliff Richard than watching me), a spot on *The Des O'Connor Show* and, of course, *Top of the Pops*, which we recorded on Wednesday for screening on Thursday. An elaborate set had been put together for us, but we fought for a simple presentation. The songs we were singing had been made by artists who just stood behind the mic and sang. There was no big band, no background distractions – they just trusted the song and we wanted to do the same. The record company tried their best to make us dance, but Jerome and I were people who sweated over clicking fingers simultaneously and we stuck by our guns.

Because it was a weekday show, Ali was working and couldn't come down to London. She was gutted because I met The Beautiful South, and she's a big fan. Watching from home in Tynemouth, she actually had a better idea of what was going on than I did. While we were still backstage, the presenters that week announced us on camera with, 'Get your granny out of the cupboard, put on your woolly sweater. We didn't put them there, you did, and we don't understand why...' Ali told me about it later and I was relieved I hadn't heard it at the time.

With the single's success came all kinds of offers: everything from opening supermarkets to voice-overs and after-dinner speeches. I'd never done it before and was taken aback by how things worked. That summer I was invited to an award

ceremony and before I had a chance to say I was happy to turn up I was offered £1000 for the effort. 'For what?' I said incredulously. 'Turning up for a three-course meal?' I obviously had a lot to learn.

I considered, then turned down, most offers. I didn't really want to go for the whole celebrity thing. After our *Top of the Pops* experience and aware of the continuing media backlash against us, I was also very wary of live appearances. One of the only exceptions I made was to appear on *An Audience with Freddie Starr*. As a child I thought he was hilarious, so I said yes. It was a big mistake which confirmed my worst suspicions.

The theatre was packed with actors, singers and people who were famous for being famous. I was with Trevor Fox, a close friend and a great northern actor. The idea of the series was to assemble a celebrity audience and have their questions to Freddie form the basis of his act. I'd been asked in advance whether I would mind asking him something but hadn't wanted to. But when I got there, I was pulled to one side and talked into it. Starr was given the list of

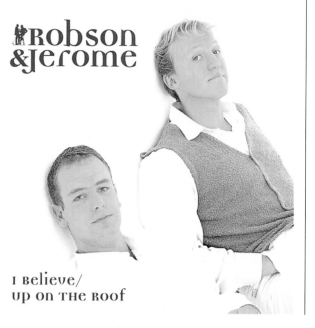

DESPERATELY TRYING TO LOOK LIKE ROCK STARS ON THE COVER OF OUR SECOND SINGLE, *I BELIEVE*.

celebrity questions in advance. Not knowing what was coming, I raised my hand as instructed.

'What do you find annoying about entertainment, Freddie?'

The pre-planned answer was swift.

'You know what I find annoying, Robson? People who con the public by covering old classics.'

On cue the band struck up with *Unchained Melody* and I realized I'd been set up.

A few people laughed nervously, but luckily very few people reacted at all. It was a pretty cheap attack on a sitting target and although it backfired on him, I felt very uncomfortable for a few minutes. The only thing that made the experience worthwhile was getting to sit next to the Tottenham player Teddy Sheringham.

Nineteen ninety-five was a crazy year and I'm only glad I was thirty when it came around. As we got swept up in the business of promotion it was easy to see why so many younger people who become an overnight pop sensation get into such a mess. Our greatest advantage was that neither of us had any intention of pursuing music beyond this. We were able call the shots while it lasted without panicking about the long-term repercussions.

In all we had three number-one singles and two chart-topping albums. After *Unchained Melody* came *I Believe*, a powerful ballad that had been a hit for Frankie Laine in the fifties and the Bachelors in the sixties before being covered by many others, including Tom Jones and Dolly Parton. It was also a favourite of my dad's and was my first choice. The B-side, chosen by Jerome, was *Up On The Roof*, a hit for The Drifters in the sixties and later covered by James Taylor. Luckily we have very similar taste in music and rarely disagreed about what we were going to sing.

I Believe wasn't released until I returned from filming in South Africa, but it followed the same trajectory as *Unchained Melody*, superseding it as fastest-selling single and breaking a handful of other records along the way. The album too went straight in at number one. It must have been an odd time for Paul McCartney. While the newly released Beatles collection *Anthology* was pushed into the number-two slot by our album *Robson and Jerome*, he also owned the rights to *Unchained Melody*.

WHAT BECOMES OF THE BROKEN HEARTED
SATURDAY NIGHT AT THE MOVIES
YOU'LL NEVER WALK ALONE

robson & jerome

The final single was *What Becomes Of The Broken Hearted*, a great old Jimmy Ruffin single, with The Drifters' *Saturday Night At The Movies* on the B-side. It stayed at number one for two weeks, as did our second album, *Take Two*. Even the videos were hits. We couldn't put a foot wrong – at least not with the public.

MORE RELAXED WITH THE RETRO LOOK. *ABOVE:* A **PUBLICITY SHOT FOR THE ALBUM** *ROBSON AND JEROME.* **OPPOSITE: THE COVER FOR OUR THIRD SINGLE,** *WHAT BECOMES OF THE BROKEN HEARTED/SATURDAY NIGHT AT THE MOVIES.*

As predictable as our record sales were the unrelenting attacks from the press, radio DJs and music commentators. For the most part, we were able to shrug these off because we saw ourselves as actors, not pop stars, but I couldn't help being surprised by the viciousness of the criticism. When *I Believe* came out, Chris Evans announced that two terrible things had happened that week: the assassination of Itzhak Rabin and the release of Robson and Jerome's new single. Were we really that bad? I wondered. Surely no one is *that* bad. Even my own paper, the *Guardian*, gave us a kicking in its 'Pass Notes' column, describing us as 'boring and talentless'. Once the bandwagon was rolling everyone hopped on.

We came along at a time when the music industry was complaining about low record sales and in theory they should have welcomed us with open arms. I guess the music media is used to setting the agenda or at least being at the forefront of the music scene. We had come out of left field, from another industry, we were unashamedly populist and we were deeply uncool: old by pop standards and singing an old song bought by a lot of older people. If anything irritated me it was the implication that music isn't for everybody, just for an *NME*-reading, elitist youth market; this I interpreted as an insult to the people who were buying the records. If the criticism had come from the public it would have worried me a lot more.

The way I dealt with it was to be as upfront about the whole thing as possible. The songs were straightforward covers of well-known classics. There was no attempt to claim them as our own. We had no musical aspirations, we weren't wannabe pop stars and what happened came directly as a result of acting.

Before the release of *I Believe* I had briefly returned to my day job, leaving the chaos of the music business behind and flying to Pretoria, in South Africa, to finish *Soldier Soldier*. It was odd

In Australia I'd been shocked by the ongoing effects of racism, but in Africa I saw racism so widespread, so deeply ingrained and so socially acceptable, it made Australia look liberal. I was looking at the results of generations of indoctrination and saw a black population that was not just looked down on but dismissed as beneath consideration.

By contrast, the country itself was marvellous and I was left with some wonderful memories of the place. Our days started early. The light was short and to catch the sun rise we were usually on set at four or five in the morning. Turning up on set to see blue wildebeests grazing as the sun rises on a beautiful national park was an incredible experience. We saw animals crossing our path that we had only ever seen through the bars of a cage.

On the third day we did a scene in which the platoon is sent out to build a medical centre. A civil war is in progress, the local area has been bombed and the regiment is on hand with manpower, resources and engineering expertise. It was a big scene involving hundreds of extras, mostly women. As we were about to start shooting it struck the director that singing would make a great background to the scene and the women were asked if there was anything they could all sing. On cue, four hundred women began to sing. It an incredible impact and

flying out without Jerome for the first time. Half the reason we'd stuck with it so long was because we knew it would be fun working together. One of us would say, 'Go on, let's do another' and the other would say, 'Oh, all right then.' This time I was on my own.

was so moving that Razaak Adoti, one of the black actors, just broke down. We had to stop filming. The sound of hundreds of voices singing such a beautiful song just floored us. From then on we used songs as a backdrop, closing one episode with the emotional ANC anthem, *Nkosi Sikelel'i Afrika*.

actor and just as rewarding to see the programme get the feedback it deserved. Then it was back to South Africa to say goodbye to Tucker. There were various suggestions on how he should make his big exit. I favoured killing him off, but the scriptwriters came up with a less dramatic solution. He is standing by the sea in South Africa, the setting is gorgeous and in theory everything should be right with the world. But Tucker is lost. His relationship with Donna is on the rocks. Tired of army life, she has gone off and got an education and, during long periods without Tucker, has become increasingly independent. Tucker, on the

The chance to travel as I did with *Soldier Soldier* was an unexpected bonus. I gained from my insight into other cultures in a way I had never expected. Nana Sarah may not have made it to the countries she told us about in her stories, but I had been luckier. When *Soldier Soldier* started there hadn't exactly been a rush from the acting fraternity to get into the series. The subject matter probably put off a lot of people, although war, guns and violence were never, in fact, the focus of the series. By the end of series four every bugger wanted to be on it.

Ali came out to visit me this time. We knew it might be a while before I'd have the opportunity to travel with my work again. Years earlier she had left home to study and she's very independent, so I didn't worry about her finding something to do. She'd come out to the set and write or paint. For me it was enough just having her there.

We also saw each other again in London when I called back between episodes to pick up an award. Television viewers had voted me best television actor and *Soldier Soldier* had won the National Television Award for most popular drama. It was great to know the public were still with me as an

other hand, has nothing to fall back on. While Donna has created a new life which she is ready to step into, he hasn't moved forward and he doesn't know where the future is going for him. So they part. He says goodbye to her and walks out of shot.

Although it made perfect sense within the scheme of things, it was an anticlimax for the audience, particularly in the north-east, where the final episode had received a fair bit of hype. After trailers flagging the big night – 'Well, it's goodbye Tucker in tonight's *Soldier Soldier*' – expectations were high. My dad expected a shoot-out and Kate, my agent, had romantic visions of him walking hopelessly out to sea. When I just turned with the parting words 'Look after Macauley' and walked off screen, there was a chorus of 'What was all that about then, man?'

For me it was hard to believe it was all over. I'd spent the past five years in Tucker's shoes. I'd travelled the world as part of the *Soldier Soldier* entourage and worked year in year out with the same tight-knit group of actors. Now I had some serious thinking to do about where I was going next.

CHAPTER ELEVEN

We started to think about moving from Tynemouth sometime in 1996. Although Jerome and I had been in the public eye for a while, Ali and I had started to attract a lot more press attention over the past year. Even our families learned to be cautious. Ali's mum had been tracked down via the phone book in the early days of our marriage and chatted politely for twenty minutes before being told she was being taped and would be quoted. She's now so careful that even some of Ali's closest relatives don't know where she lives. At home Ali took the brunt of it, with journalists frequently following her home from work and wedging a foot in the door if they got the chance. As soon as she saw a Pentax from the

GOING IT ALONE

upstairs window she knew what was coming.

'How do you feel about Robson and Jerome being so friendly?' was one common opener. This line of questioning stemmed from an interview I had given the *Sun* in which I said: '...men are not supposed to love each other but I love my mate Jerome.' This was said in the context of encouraging men to be more expressive to each other and I meant it. Jerome and I thought nothing of it, but the tabloids went to town. Soon after, we appeared in a photo spread with our arms around each other and my head resting on Jerome's shoulder – shock horror! Press speculation ranged from the notion that it was a publicity stunt to the assumption that we were gay. It was extraordinary.

Once Ali made it clear that she wasn't going to be drawn on the subject of my 'close relationship' with Jerome, conversation would usually turn to her own private life and the less willing she was to discuss it, the more fascinated the press became. There was nothing to hide and it wouldn't have made good copy anyway.

RELAXING AT HOME IN NORTHUMBERLAND.

For most of that period she was working with the terminally ill and to have talked about work would have been a breach of confidence. Not only would it have been a gross intrusion for the people she was working with, but it would also have seriously altered the relationship she had built up with them as Alison Ogilvie, not Mrs Robson Green.

Nineteen ninety-six was shaping up to be another busy year. I was keeping my eye out for a good television drama and had two Coastal Productions (Citizen Films had become Coastal Productions in 1992) projects on the go: a theatre piece I was working on with Max Roberts called *The Beautiful Game* and a two-hour musical drama for television called *Ain't Misbehavin'*.

Ain't Misbehavin' wasn't due to start filming until April, but we'd already started pre-production talks before going to Australia. Jerome and I wanted to make a popular, accessible drama, a version of the kind of thing I loved as a kid, incorporating light comedy, music and romance. After we discussed it with Norman Stone the story began to come together. He hit on the idea of combining a romantic story-line with the big band sound and we realized the obvious solution was to set it during the war. Trying to recreate the atmosphere of those years appealed to me. I imagined it as a time when emotions were intensified by the situation. People lived in fear – for their own lives and the lives of the men they had seen off to war – and this manifested itself as a kind of recklessness. People fell in love quickly and intensely, they took risks because there might be no tomorrow and strong friendships were forged in the face of adversity.

From there, things moved quickly, probably too quickly. One minute we were scribbling notes on a napkin over a pub lunch and the next we were pitching a very vague idea to the network. I didn't have a clue what

I was doing, but I was in and out before I had a chance to worry about it.

'Two guys – snazzy suits and good hats – and they're in a big band.'

'Do you sing in it?'

'Yep.'

'Fine, no problem.'

It was too easy. With hindsight I guess they saw us as virtually risk-free. With the records selling like hot cakes and *Soldier Soldier* still on air, we could do no wrong, and as far as they were concerned they had Robson and Jerome doing what people liked them doing best: playing romantic heroes *and* singing. We got the go-ahead before I went to Africa and they couldn't advance us the money fast enough. If I'd known then what I know now I might have binned the napkin and forgotten the whole thing.

The Beautiful Game also came about in a pub. Max and I often went to matches together and the idea was born out of that shared interest. It start-ed with an evening talking football in the Baltic, a pub near the Live Theatre. We were chatting about the players and organizers at Newcastle United, some of whom I'd got to know quite well. TV opens doors and after the success of *Soldier Soldier* I had been invited to the directors' box to watch Newcastle. Meeting the players was the biggest thrill; I might as well have been a skinny ten-year-old all over again. The mere presence of people like Alan Shearer and Kevin Keegan reduced me to a gibbering wreck and if they actually spoke to me I could barely string a sentence together.

As Max and I sat and talked about our mutual love of the game we reached the same conclusion: it would make a great play. At that time Newcastle were winning the Premier League, with Keegan at the helm, and a family-based drama about the club's history seemed timely. The idea was simply to celebrate football, in particular the relationship between fans and club. It was also an attempt to

WITH WRITER MICHAEL CHAPLIN AT THE OPENING NIGHT OF *THE BEAUTIFUL GAME* AT THE THEATRE ROYAL IN NEWCASTLE.

enough excuse. A cast was brought together, including my mate Trevor, another fan, and Denise Welch, a great actress I had worked with on *Soldier Soldier*. We were ready to go.

We opened in the summer of 1996. The first night was packed and the whole Newcastle team showed up, which gave us all a great lift. But, despite good review, it didn't last. In the time it had taken for us to put the play together the tide had turned against the Magpies. Cantona was performing miracles for Manchester United and Spurs beat Newcastle in an all-important game, leaving the way open for Man U to take the trophy. What should have been a celebration turned into a period of mourning in Newcastle. Tynesiders suffered and so did *The Beautiful Game*.

In the end it didn't do the business we'd hoped. We couldn't have anticipated the fortunes of the club, but there were other problems that we should have been aware of. At the Live Theatre Max always went to great lengths to involve everyone concerned with promoting a play. Everyone from the actors to the bar staff was consulted in the belief that they knew the play better than anyone else. On this occasion none of us was part of the process and as a consequence we didn't manage to appeal to the right audience in the right way. You live and learn.

For me, and probably for Max, it was a lost opportunity. There was something I wanted to communicate about football and if you don't draw the crowds you can't get the message across. It's a old cliché, but I really believe football is more than a game. For me and many people like me, it's an incredibly emotional experience and a part of life I feel passionately about. Just watching the team come out of the tunnel at Wembley is enough to make me weep.

There is a negative side. Racism and violence are something I see yet don't understand, but with more black players and people like Keegan speaking

explain to non-fans what the game means, why it inspires such loyalty and devotion. Within an hour we had the outline and rang Michael Chaplin the same night to see if he'd write it. Max had been an admirer of Michael's father, Sid Chaplin, since first coming to Newcastle, and when he later commissioned an adaptation of Sid's stories he met the rest of Sid's family, including Michael. Like his father, Michael was a good writer and, equally important, he was another Newcastle fan.

It was decided that Max would direct and Coastal would produce. The venue would be Newcastle's best, the Theatre Royal. Max had directed there the previous year and Alan Plater's play, *Shooting the Legend*, starring Trevor Fox and Tim Healy, did so well that they were keen to have Max return with another production.

What followed was a fantastic period of research for Max and Michael which involved learning as much as possible about the history of the club, as well as meeting the players. I missed a lot of the best bits because I was busy and as co-producer and part-financer I didn't really have a good

out against the worst elements of the game, the climate is starting to change for the better. Beyond that there is a very positive side: the emotion within a stadium which can bring people together like nothing else. I've been at matches where there have been silences to mark both Hillsborough and Dunblane. The whistle is blown and the cheering and barracking stop, the scraps and drinking stop, little kids are shushed and the silence is deafening. Losing a premiership isn't tragic. People going before their time, that's tragic.

We hadn't managed it this time, but a football story was something I knew I would come back to when the time was right. In the spring of the same year, filming was due to begin on *Ain't Misbehavin'*. We had an amazing cast, including Jane Lapotaire, Warren Mitchell, George Melly, Julia Sawalha and Jim Carter, and the script had been written by Bob Larby, the man behind *The Good Life*.

The story-line had been tightened up, but Romy and I needed to find a character. Got it! He would be Eddie Wallis with an 'is' and I would be Eric Van Trapp. Working on the names took about three weeks, leaving two days to deal with character development, character journey and motivation. As usual, Jerome got to play the good guy, Eddie, who has been discharged from the RAF after being injured in a heroic crash-landing over France. He would like to be on the front line fighting fascism but can't, so instead he takes his chances as a saxophonist in the Ray Smiles Big

DISCUSSING A SCRIPT OVER BREAKFAST WITH TIM HEALY.

104

Band. My character, Eric, couldn't be more different. He's a charming Jack-the-Lad who has managed to avoid conscription and is making the most out of the war, trading in black-market goods, which he hides in his double-bass case. The two characters collide when they end up playing for the same band.

It all seemed so simple at first, but it wasn't long before I realized the problems involved with acting *and* producing. As an independent production company, we had been given a hefty proportion of the budget upfront. The rest we had to find ourselves, through distribution deals, merchandising and anything else we could come up with, and it would be refunded at the end of the project. The appropriate staff had been put in place and, as far as I was concerned, they were taking care of it. But within a matter of weeks we realized we had a problem. The distribution deals weren't sewn up as we thought, intellectual property rights weren't in place and the merchandising was a shambles. These were all things which could bring money into the company to underwrite the bank loan we had taken to cover the shortfall, and the bank wasn't handing over a penny without some security.

Filming was already well underway by the time we realized how serious our financial problems were. Suddenly we found we had actors' wages to pay, a crew to pay, a scriptwriter to keep happy – and we had no cash to do it. I did the only thing I could to keep it afloat: I put in a lot of my own money and together Jerome and I underwrote the rest of the bank loan. It was serious bread, but without it we would have ground to a halt. It was too late to worry about the mistakes that had already been made and who was responsible. By now the ball was rolling and there was no stopping it.

Although the filming lasted only six weeks, the whole project, from pre-production to post-production, took much longer. We filmed mainly in the south of England and central London. Trying to film a period piece in 1990s London was a nightmare. Jerome and I spent a lot of time in an old motorbike and side-car and the design team would spend hours setting up the sequence – preparing sets, period cars and costumes. On cue we'd zoom off past a terrace of houses and suddenly we'd hit a set of traffic lights and get carried off down a one-way system. Another thing we had overlooked was the school opposite the location. Every day at three-thirty sharp, filming would be halted by high-pitched screams: 'Wahhhh, there's Robson and Jerome.' It was pandemonium.

Halfway through filming it emerged that we had another problem that was harder to control than a mob of hormonal teenagers. *Ain't Misbehavin'* had been pitched as a two-hour drama and that's what the budget was based on. Gradually we realized we had a three-hour drama in the making and not enough cash to cover it. Not only was it going to cost a lot more than planned, but worse, we had been scheduled on network TV for two hours and now we had three. The obvious solution was to cut it, but we tried and it just didn't make any sense. We'd gone too far down the line to backtrack. This kind of thing had always been someone else's problem; now it was mine.

Things began to snowball. The three-hour length also meant we couldn't sell it abroad, as they buy in two-hour packages. Distribution deals

LEARNING MY LINES AT THE HEARTBREAK SOUP CAFÉ ON THE QUAYSIDE.

started to fall through and we started to panic. 'We'll merchandise like mad,' we decided. 'We'll have Robson and Jerome calendars, T-shirts and scratch cards, even bloody Robson and Jerome pillowcases.'

LEFT: **MAKING MY ESCAPE IN** *AIN'T MISBEHAVIN'*. *ABOVE:* **WAITING FOR THE CAMERAS TO ROLL ON SET.**

I was livid. Here we were trying to raise money in a frenzy when it should have all been taken care of at the beginning. The budget was spiralling, the actors' agents were renegotiating for more money because the programme was longer, the scheduling was a mess and we still didn't have any money. I was angry with myself – ultimately I had to shoulder the responsibility for the people I'd hired – and I was terrified; by this time I thought I was going to lose our home in Tynemouth. It was time to call in the big guns. Somehow, and I'm not sure how, Sandra, my financial adviser, sorted it all out. She'd come a long way since our first meeting and there was nothing she couldn't handle. Distribution deals were rejigged, the network was pacified and a deal was struck to release a soundtrack from *Ain't Misbehavin'*. We all breathed a huge sigh of relief.

It wasn't easy to put the money worries to one side, but when we did we had a lot of fun. Filming and recording the big band scenes was fantastic and there were some great discoveries – Warren Mitchell was actually in a big band and it turned out he could play a mean clarinet – and some surprises – George Melly was a genius but pretty hard of hearing, which caused havoc until we figured out how to work around it in the big music scenes.

In retrospect, though, the good bits are eclipsed by the money worries. Financial security is important to me. I'd gone without and seen my parents go without, but when the fifth series of *Soldier Soldier* and the singles had come along, my financial adviser was able to give me the reassurance I needed. 'We can work this out so that you won't ever be in the situation you always feared,' she told me, 'a long time poor. We'll not blow it and you'll know after this that whatever happens in the future you'll be OK.' When *Ain't Misbehavin'* seemed to be putting all that at risk I was under terrible pressure. I had wanted it to work and for people to enjoy themselves making it. Instead, I was completely uptight about the money. At one point I was acting in a fight scene in a nightclub and all I could think of was the number of chairs getting trashed and how much it was costing. I made a mental note to think long and hard before both acting and producing again.

As *Ain't Misbehavin'* drew to a close, Jerome and I knew it was time to cut the cord. We were so closely associated in the public mind that people would point me out in the street when I was alone and say, 'Look, there's Robson and Jerome.'

I know it was the same for Romy. The off-screen relationship between us was a matter of choice but the on-screen double act was never planned. We thought things would change when we quit *Soldier Soldier*, but when the singles had taken off like Exocets it had just consolidated our joined-at-the-hip image. Like Jerome, I was just waiting for the right part to come along.

As soon as I heard the story-line for *Reckless* I knew it was the one. I could picture myself in it from the start. It was an old-fashioned love story and the man behind it was Paul Abbott, whose work on *Cracker* had been excellent. It couldn't have been more straightforward. They knew they wanted me, so I didn't need to audition and we could start work that August.

The part was a young doctor who falls in love with an older woman, but it wasn't so much the age factor that I saw as the story as his own personal dilemma. She is married to his boss, and pursuing the relationship may have terrible consequences for both of them; he knows there will be sacrifices to be made in terms of his career and his relationships with his father, friends and colleagues. It's a dilemma of his own making, but at the same time the situation is out of his control because he is in love and can't give her up.

Reckless lived up to all my expectations. The director, Dave Richards, was one of the best I'd worked with and his close friendship with Paul Abbott made for a warm atmosphere on set. Being an old romantic himself, Dave used a lot of long-lens shots, which meant there was no one in your face and scenes could unfold in a more intimate and real way. At the same time, he didn't stand back behind the lens and watch the monitor, as many directors do. He was right up there with us, watching and advising.

Dave's sensitive approach and Paul's great writing paid off. The audience feedback was great. The press reception, on the other hand, was mixed. The broadsheets showed a lot of interest and I was chuffed to bits to read positive pieces in the *Guardian* and the *Independent*. But the *Mail* and the *Mirror* destroyed it and the slant was as personal as ever. There were plenty of joky digs about my tendency to get my kit off, but there was also a sense that I was a working-class boy who had got above himself; I was acceptable with my regional accent and Geordie attitude as a porter or a soldier, but a doctor was different.

The reaction was partly a reluctance to accept me in a new role; but although this happens to all

IN BED WITH CO-STAR FRANCESCA ANNIS IN *RECKLESS*.

CO-STAR MICHAEL KITCHEN
AND I FIGHT OVER THE
GIRL IN RECKLESS.

A SOMBRE MOMENT DURING THE FILMING OF *TOUCHING EVIL* FOR MERIDIAN TV.

myself at first, was the house. The terrible ongoing debt of a mortgage was what had crippled my parents, so it was a big thing for me to buy the house outright. I'd always known that the rewards for surviving as an actor were high, but even as I started to earn more, and in theory had to worry less about the future, there was always the feeling that some bastard would come along and take everything away. Owning my own house didn't quite put an end to that feeling but at least I knew I could give that bastard a run for his money now.

As we moved into 1997 I had two more promising projects on the go. The first was *Touching Evil*, a six-part psychological drama about a crack

actors, in my case it was compounded by a refusal to allow me to cross certain boundaries. I didn't take it too seriously. As long as the public were watching, I knew they liked it and if they liked it, I could ignore the rest.

Somehow, in the middle of all the chaos, Ali and I had managed to move house that spring. The new house was all I had hoped it would be, even if I wasn't there for more than two weeks at a stretch during that first year. It was remote, quiet enough to hear the birds sing, and overlooked some of the most stunning countryside in Northumberland, with not a single house to spoil the view. The house was *Unchained Melody*: the bricks-and-mortar result of our brief fling with the music business, and it made all the hassle worthwhile. There had been a time when even friends were saying, 'Rob, man, I saw you on bloody *Surprise, Surprise* the other night singing some old rubbish. What're you up to, man?' Well, the answer, even if I didn't know it

team of undercover cops whose job it is to track down serial killers. Maybe it had been worth going through all those gruelling interviews a few years earlier because it was as the result of one of them that the part of DC Creegan came my way. I'd tried for a part in *Stay Lucky* and was so overwhelmed by the presence of Dennis Waterman from the *Minder* of my childhood that I fell to pieces. I didn't get the part, but the executive producer, Vernon Lawrence, had remembered me and this new one was mine without the ordeal of an audition.

Touching Evil was a great opportunity to do something different. It was a serious drama series that confronted the darker side of life, taking on subjects like child murder and euthanasia. The story-lines, some based on real cases, were fascinating and I knew the role was just what I had been looking for. To my relief – given the subject matter – it was low on blood and guts and in no way was violence normalized or glamorized. The emphasis was on a network of relationships: between the individuals in the police team, between the police and criminals and between

Creegan and his family. I knew it was something I could do well.

After the first episode was screened I got a fax from my dad: 'Robson, you're leaving yourself very little room for improvement.' I knew *Touching Evil* wouldn't get the viewing figures of *Soldier Soldier*, but whatever the critics had planned for the next morning's papers I felt it was the best thing I'd done so far.

As filming ended on *Touching Evil* I had a two-week break before heading back to London to get started on *The Prince of Hearts*. Spending time at home was a luxury I'd missed over the past year and now I was there I wanted to make the most of it. I would often wake early and head downstairs for some tea. After life on set, there was nothing as relaxing as the view across the hills at six in the morning with not another soul in sight. Just me, a couple of hungry rock sparrows and Ali sleeping peacefully upstairs.

Most nights we stayed at home and just enjoyed being together again while it lasted. Going out could be more trouble than it was worth as we discovered when we went out one night for a drink. After half an hour spent signing autographs I went to the toilet and as I shut the door to the cubicle I heard two guys come in.

'Do you see who's in tonight?' a voice said. 'That fuckin' wanker who canna shoot coal.'

Translated from Geordie, that meant I couldn't sing. It comes from the days when men used to sell coal in the street and shouted, 'Coal. Coal'. I was that bad I couldn't even shout, 'Coal'.

'And he's a shite actor,' added his mate for good measure.

From my cubicle, I joined in, giving it my best trainspotter voice. 'Well, actually, I think Robson Green's a marvellous singer, I do.'

'You what!' the voice came back.

'Absolutely marvellous,' I wittered. 'What's that song he sings? "I believe for every drop of rain that falls, a flower grows..." What a

wonderful philosophy of life.'

'Who the hell are you – some sort of weirdo, man?'

'No,' I answered, reverting to my own voice. 'I'm that wanker who canna shoot coal.'

Before we knew it I was on my way back to London for *The Prince of Hearts*. I don't think I was the first choice for the part of Barry Grimes, but once we got started it fitted like a glove. I played the bodyguard responsible for the heir to the throne and the chemistry felt great between me, Rupert Penry-Jones as the Prince and Tara Fitzgerald as the American student we both fall for. It was nice to get back to light comedy and Rupert was a natural.

Filming began in April, in and around Cambridge, where the Prince and Grace are studying. One of our first scenes took place on a rugby field, alongside real and very large rugby players, some of them internationals. They

WITH CO-STAR NICOLA WALKER DURING THE MAKING OF *TOUCHING EVIL*.

BY THE RIVER CAM IN CAMBRIDGE WITH TARA FITZGERALD AND RUPERT PENRY-JONES DURING THE FILMING OF THE PRINCE OF HEARTS.

needed the scene to be set and the director filled them in. 'Rupert Penry-Jones is a prince and, well, basically you lot don't like him. In fact, you think he's a right wanker.' They all nodded seriously. 'Robson Green,' he went on, 'is the Prince's bodyguard… ' The laughter started as soon as he mentioned the word 'bodyguard'; soon they were hysterical and next they went into a rendition of *Unchained Melody*. Revenge is sweet, though. As I was leaving, a huge prop forward sidled up, out of sight of the team, and whispered, 'Could I have an autograph

for my granny?' 'An autograph for your granny,' I yelled, immediately prompting a second chorus, this time: 'Our prop forward's a poofta.'

Like *Reckless*, *The Prince of Hearts* had a high feelgood factor and the feeling on set was the same. But unusually the off-set chat wasn't shop talk: the subject on everyone's mind was the general election due the following month. I managed to get home for the big night and we decided to stay put and watch the results come through on the telly. We had considered heading to the nearest Labour Party gathering, but the memory of the last time was too awful. I had backed Kinnock and canvassed a bit. There was a good vibe around the country, reinforced by encouraging opinion polls, and after that the slide from optimism to loss was terrible. I remembered the Basildon result as if it was yesterday. As soon as I saw the triumphant smile on the MP's face, I knew the Tories were back in.

This time around it was hard to imagine Labour could win, but by ten o'clock Ali was on her way to the local shop for a bottle of champagne. Like everyone else around the country, we channel-hopped through the stations, taking in the early results. First Basildon, then Birmingham Edgbaston, followed by Portsmouth – one after another the successes came through for Labour. The Tories were well and truly ousted. I was so happy I cried.

It was incredible to think that there were people in their twenties who had lived their entire adult lives under a Tory government and that this would finally change. They say if voting changed anything they'd abolish it, but after Blair's victory I felt something had changed, because people had found their voice and made it happen. There was a feeling in the air of a new beginning, and I went to bed a happy man.

CHAPTER TWELVE

People sometimes ask what goes through an actor's mind before he goes on stage or on camera. It's fear – fear at the most basic level, especially when you're starting out in your career. It's the fear that you won't get the words out when you hear someone shout 'Action'. The fear that fifteen million people will be watching you on network television or, even worse, the fear that they won't. So why would anyone go through such a harrowing process again and again? In my case there's always been an inherent need to stand up in front of the nearest group of people and entertain them. It's the way I express myself and I don't think I could suppress it if I tried. I do it on screen and off and it's been that way since I was old enough to talk.

LOOKING FORWARD, GLANCING BACK

Although my career started in theatre, television was my first love. It captivated me as a child and as an adult I'm still bowled over by the power it has to make me laugh, cry or leap out of my seat as a ball soars towards an open goal. Television is accessible in a way that theatre isn't. It's the most democratic of mediums and I feel very lucky to have found my place in it. I didn't go to public school and I didn't go to drama school. If I had, I might take things for granted. As it is, I know I might never have met Max and left the shipyard. I might never have left Newcastle for *Casualty* or *Casualty* for *Soldier Soldier* and the chance to travel the world. Coming from a mining village like Dudley, I took none of these things for granted.

The circumstances of my life have been changed dramatically by television, yet I am still the same person. The parts that have worked best are those that have allowed me to play an extension of myself and recognizing this has allowed me to make the right choices. Early theatre parts tended to be working-class Geordies because the plays were written by local writers. When television came along, it was a bigger playing field, but with roles like Jimmy and Tucker instinct told me what I did best and I was lucky to find directors who let me do it.

I've always been driven to move forward and it's not just a career strategy: it's a personal thing. I have had offers all along the way to return to *Casualty* and *Soldier Soldier*, to go back to making records and most recently to make a film version of *Reckless*, but I've always chosen to try something new. Some actors revisit old sets they've worked on in the same way that people go to school reunions. I've always found that odd, even uncomfortable. I'm never tempted to revisit the past. There's a strong sense in me that going back, or even staying still for too long, is a sign of failure.

If you are driven to act, there are sometimes sacrifices to be made. In my twenties I needed to be single-minded and saw marriage as something that would get in the way, kids even more so. Seeing my mam and dad trapped by a mortgage and four kids was an education. I just felt I wasn't in a position to get involved early on. I would never have left the shipyard and couldn't have survived the bouts of unemployment in my theatre days. I certainly couldn't have travelled with *Soldier Soldier* as I did if I'd known there were kids at home wondering what their dad looked like. No live-in relationship and no kids were part of the deal and a conscious decision. Now I'm thirty-two, the shit's sorted out and I have a lot more freedom to make more choices.

Developing Coastal Productions is one of those choices. If television has given me a bit of clout, I can't think of anything I'd rather use it for than to bring employment to the north-east and to bring attention to northern writers. I can do that through

ON HOLIDAY IN A FAVOURITE SPOT, BUT WE'RE NOT SAYING WHERE.

Coastal. Unlike acting, production is an enabling role. If I come across a play or idea I like, I have the means to bring it to the stage. In the end *The Beautiful Game* didn't do the business we'd hoped for, but we weren't in it for short-term gain. We set out to raise the profile of Coastal Productions through investment in the arts and, even more importantly, investment in people, and this much we achieved.

I never quite gave up on the idea of a play about football, and *Dog Stars* is my second attempt, this time for television. The script is still being developed by Guy Pearce, but Granada are interested and if all goes well we hope to see it reach the screen as a six-part series sometime in 1998. It's a story about people, their relationships and their hopes and dreams, but behind this is an attempt to convey the joy of football and why those ninety minutes are so important to millions of people in different countries all over the world.

The Dog Stars are a pub football team made up of guys from a working-class background who are physically past it but love the game. They are men who dreamed of being great but would never make it, and they relive their dream through the local pub team. To them, it is their Newcastle, their Chelsea, their Manchester United. In the film they reunite after fifteen years for one last game. It is to take place in Spain and, unknown to them, the outcome of the game will settle a corrupt land deal between their former manager and the manager of the opposing German team.

The action is set in the Valley of the Anarchists in Spain's Sierra Nevada, where the last stand against Franco was fought. People from the north of England have been well liked there since 1936, when many came from Newcastle and Liverpool to fight with the anarchists against Franco, who was part of the wave of fascism then sweeping Europe. This battlefield is where the modern-day 'friendly' is to be played, and it makes for a potent meeting of English, Spanish and German cultures.

As we continue to develop *Dog Stars* we're also working on a television play called *No Regrets*, which has strong personal associations for me. It's based on an incident that took place in Dudley during the 1926 strike, when thirty miners derailed the *Flying Scotsman* on the main London

to Edinburgh line. The union members driving the train were considered scabs and the miners, thinking the train was carrying coal, meant to stop it getting through. In fact, the train was carrying two hundred and thirty passengers.

The headlines the next day were sensational and misleading, claiming some people had been killed and many seriously injured. Fortunately, the train had been travelling at only five miles per hour and no one was badly hurt. Nevertheless, the incident precipitated the end of the General Strike.

Eight men were jailed and one of them, William Muckle, remained wrongly imprisoned for many years until his wife Jenny proved in court that eight men could not have lifted the rail and that her husband was simply a scapegoat. When Muckle was released there was a

JOANNA, ME, MAM, DAVID AND DAWN AT MAM'S FOR SUNDAY LUNCH.

huge demonstration in Trafalgar Square and Jenny made a beautiful and very moving speech. So while *No Regrets* is a slice of social history, it's also a very human story of a woman's vow to free her man.

After his release, Muckle wrote his story and many years later Max came across it and showed it to me, convinced it would make a great drama. His patience paid off because we have commissioned Michael Chaplin to write it and are now in the process of raising the money.

Max Roberts is just as much of an influence today as he was when he dragged me along to youth theatre at the age of sixteen. I still go to him for advice and asked him to read scripts for *Reckless* and *Touching Evil* because I value his opinion. It was reassuring to know he rated each as a 'class act'. His advice is always the same: 'approach something with a genuine ideological perspective and you can't go wrong', and his own work provides the best example of this.

Max's aim hasn't wavered. The Live Theatre is about trying to make good theatre more accessible by reconnecting art and entertainment. The plays are by local writers and make sense to local audiences in a way that the classics never would. His latest production, a modern reworking of the York Mystery Plays, fell into two overlapping halves: the first collection of plays looked back at Tyneside's past and the second at the post-industrial landscape and the legacy of Thatcherism. While the plays are deeply bound up with politics, they are human stories about what goes on in the lives of ordinary people in the north-east. Underpinning Max's work is a belief that you have to recognize the past in order to understand the present, a notion that is especially relevant in the north-east.

Tynesiders have an unusually strong regional identity. Geographically, we're out on a limb and we're brought up with a strong sense of place. The imposing Tyne Bridge is the heart of the city and means a lot to Tynesiders, and the river itself has a great pull which keeps people coming back. Like me, both Trevor Fox and Joe Caffrey spent time in London. Although they enjoyed it, they always knew they would come back. Now Trevor has bought a house five hundred yards from the one where he was born. My mates are the same ones I've had since my days in youth theatre and a love of the area is something we all have in common.

The other thing we share is a love of performance and most of the people I came up with at the Live Theatre have stayed with it and done well. After college Joe worked on a few Films on Four and *Spender* and most recently appeared in the reworked Mystery Plays at the Live Theatre. Trevor began work as an education worker in community theatre around the time his son Charlie was born, but missed acting so much that he came back to it. He now has a seven-year-old son, so it's tough, but he loves the work as much as ever and regularly appears at the Live

RELAXING AT HOME.

Theatre. Steve Chambers writes a lot for radio and his latest theatre play, *Pub Fiction*, was one of those which made the biggest impact as part of the Mysteries.

My own ties with the Live Theatre have changed, but they are still strong. Acting has been replaced by a role in production and alongside that I do what I can to encourage new actors. I love to be able to talk in schools and say, 'I went to a great youth theatre, right here in Newcastle. I travelled to Germany and the Edinburgh Festival and had my eyes opened by the experience.' I find it easy to talk with conviction about the power of theatre because I believe passionately in the idea. By way of example I sometimes talk about the way theatres were closed down with the rise of fascism because of their power to inform and educate through entertainment. Of course, the only question most twelve-year-olds want to ask is how many actresses I get to snog, but there are always one or two who feel like I did at that age and are encouraged.

Drama was the only way of expressing myself as a child and I was lucky to find people in my own community who nurtured it. There is no drama school in the north-east at the moment and youth theatre is struggling. Last year we were awarded money from Northern Arts and the National Lottery, enough to fund three young actors to work on productions at the Live Theatre for a year. It's a tiny contribution, but it's enormously satisfying. The next step would be to fund a youth theatre where thirty to forty actors could study for a year. It would be a huge breakthrough and if Coastal does well next year we can consider it.

I'd like kids to see acting as a viable alternative and to understand that you don't have to be the product of a London drama school to pursue it. The same applies to writing. A lot of the characters

UPSTAIRS AT HOME SHORTLY AFTER LABOUR'S MONUMENTAL VICTORY, WORKING AND WATCHING TONY BLAIR MAKE HIS FIRST SPEECH AS PRIME MINISTER ON THE TELLY.

I've played celebrate the people and culture of the north-east and I have good local writers to thank for those parts. The plays I'm developing with Coastal reflect the same desire to celebrate where I come from and the idiosyncrasies of the people who live there. Every single person has a story to tell and if you look at drama as representing people's lives as honestly as you can, it demystifies the whole thing. Don't do, be. It's the oldest acting cliché in the book.

The beauty of Newcastle is that the writers are there just waiting for someone to give them a voice. The tragedy is that many aren't heard beyond the north-east, and few have waited longer than Tom Hadaway. The playwrights' society founded by Tom all those years ago now has a hundred and forty members competing for work in a handful of venues. The problem, says Tom, is that the work, his own included, doesn't get the chance to travel. He has worked with award-winning directors like Jack Gold and Alistair Reid, who used local talent while filming in the north but then went home again. As a younger man he was motivated to see this change but age is catching up with him. He feels a bit defeated by the way theatre is now driven by money managers who have become the new arbiters of public taste. He should be bitter about the indifference of the south, but it's not in his nature. He's too gentle and too modest to push for the place he should have as a writer. Of himself, he'll say, 'I'm not really very bright, to tell the truth. People think

ENJOYING THE LOCAL BEACHES ON A GLORIOUS SUNNY DAY.

OUT FISHING WTH FERN, WHO ALWAYS CATCHES MORE THAN ME.

you must be if you write plays, but most of my work is based on characters I've met and situations I've known. I only act as a medium – there's a real social situation on the one hand and the dramatic interpretation on the other – but there's nothing very clever about what I do. They say the best writing is where the writer is least evident and I tend to let the characters write themselves.'

Tom has since had a stroke. He seems frail now and I miss the days when I would call round for him and take him to a match, but he remains one of my closest friends and a great inspiration.

It is ironic that the place I worked so hard to escape from is one I would never leave now. I love Newcastle and the people who mean most to me are all here. It was only ever the circumstances I

wanted to leave behind, not the place, and the person I am is too tightly bound up with where I come from for me to contemplate leaving.

My relationship with my family is very important and they are in Newcastle, so Newcastle is still home. I was always close to my mam and that hasn't changed. It's taken longer to get to that stage with my dad, although the relationship has grown steadily. He admits now he was strict; when I bared my backside in *Reckless* his first comment was 'I've belted that arse a thousand times' – and it was true. But he stands by his methods and when I look at the four of us now, I suppose we've all turned out OK, so between them my mam and dad must have been on the right track.

Dad stopped work after the miners' strike in 1984. He breathed fresh air for the first time and never went back, accepting redundancy at fifty. With the money he pursued one of his own dreams and bought himself a racehorse. He'd always loved horses, something passed on by his father, who had been in the Royal Horse Artillery during his army service. It was great to see Dad smile again and our relationship today is better than ever.

We still have the same things in common. Although he says he never brought me up to be a socialist, it was just part and parcel of where I grew up and we still share the same politics. At the same time we both see that things have changed and, surprisingly, Dad is all for Blair. 'There'll be no sleaze wi' him,' he says.

Football is the other big link and we still go to matches together whenever we can. The only difference is that I'm in a position to shout him a season ticket these days instead of him paying for me. Last April we spent eight days in Monaco, along with Max and Michael Chaplin, for the Newcastle–Monaco game. The team was slaughtered, but before the game the Geordie fans struck up a new chant: 'There's only one Robson Green, only one Robson Green.' I may have been slightly embarrassed, but Dad was proud as a peacock.

Events haven't changed my parents much. Mam is still devoted to her family and her two dachshunds. She has travelled to Australia, Hong Kong and Europe over the past few years, but she's always glad to get back to her semi in Burradon. As far as Mam's concerned, things were never that bad. Everybody was in the same boat. 'You made your money and it kept you,' she says. 'You just didn't have any to spare.' What mattered to her was that we were all happy and that has never changed.

Dad, well, he's happiest at his allotment in Dudley, passed on to him by his father. He grows championship leeks – his 'bairns', he calls them – and brings me home-grown double begonias for the garden. He still takes to the stage sometimes although it's karaoke nowadays, never misses 'grab a

granny night' at the club and still goes drinking with the same mates he had twenty years ago.

All four of us inherited a strong work ethic from our parents and my brother and sisters started early and haven't stopped. Dawn stuck with hairdressing for fourteen years until our mam got a flower shop and then worked there until Mam retired. They sold the shop on the Friday and on Monday Dawn was in a new job, where she's worked as a cashier since. Only a few months ago history repeated itself and she found herself in the front row at the Live Theatre, this time watching the début of her son, Daymon. It must have brought it all back to her and I'm sure she went through the same angst as my mam when Daymon gave up his hotel job to become an actor.

Joanna went out to work at sixteen, first at the shop with Mam, then as a telephonist and telex operator for a local demolition company. Like me, she married in her late twenties, but unlike me, she stayed at home until then. She still lives no more than five minutes from Mam's house and after having a daughter

PRETENDING TO PLAY GOLF (NOTICE THE BALL NEVER LEAVES MY FEET) WITH MY FATHER-IN-LAW, BILL, AT THE NEWBIGGIN-BY-THE-SEA GOLF CLUB.

of her own, Gemma, returned to work for an insurance company.

David left school even earlier. At fifteen he started work at a farm, and loved it, but by the time he hit eighteen his mates were all out earning and he couldn't keep pace. From there he became a labourer and is now a scaffolder. We're all very different and David in particular is very different from me. He can't imagine anything worse than the job I do.

David has always kept himself to himself. He could always keep a secret, which meant he was someone to be trusted, and that's never changed. He never aspired to material things. As a kid he loved wildlife and nature and has always had a great understanding of what is precious in life.

He has recently become a father too, so they all have their own families now, but for the time being I'm happy to make Ali my priority, and as far as we are concerned, looking after our beloved Weimaraner, Fern, is enough of a responsibility. Of course, Dad still asks about 'the chances of a bambino before I pop my clogs', but so far our married life together has been short because I've been away for so much of it. At the moment we're still busy enjoying each other's company.

I'm still as full of admiration for Ali as I was when we first met. Over the years her work has involved looking after people with severe learning difficulties, spina bifida, cerebral palsy and the terminally ill, and so her perspective on life is completely different from that of anyone in my profession. She understands what I do and she enjoys entertainment as much as anyone else, but in terms of having a hold on reality she's in a different league and it's very good for both of us. Lately she's rediscovered her artistic roots. The beautiful scenery of Northumberland is an ideal setting for an artist.

All in all I'm a happy man and there's a speech at the end of *The Prince of Hearts* that sums it up well. When Barry comes to Cambridge to look after the heir to the throne he is thrown into a completely foreign environment. A man with little education himself, he is suddenly surrounded by

RELAXING WITH ALI ON A NORTHUMBRIAN SHORE.

academics, poetry and literature, but instead of reacting against it, he absorbs it and finds himself transformed by the experience. The speech takes place in a lecture theatre, where Barry, now a lecturer himself, tries to explain the process of learning and life.

'As D.H. Lawrence states in his letter to Frieda of the 7th June, 1920: "The journey of the working classes to fulfil their fullest potential must be a Journey of the Heart." So this is the point, in Shakespeare as much as in Lawrence, the most ordinary lives are extraordinary not because of what we are given but because of what we are able to achieve.'

When I took Dad up to see the new house for the first time we stood side by side on a bank and looked out over the Simonside Hills. He asked whether I'd ever thought I would end up buying something like this and I realized it was a hard question to answer. I'd grown up on a council estate in Dudley and however much I learned from growing up there, I did want out – out of the economic trap if not the community. There's a myth that you have to come from a working-class background to understand what it's like to struggle, but I don't agree. To live on tick with the wallpaper peeling off is horrible and everyone knows how it feels not to want to repeat a bad experience. Yes, I had wanted to end up with a different life, but no, I don't think I realized I would succeed. When I look back, I know I've come a long way, but I've brought the values of the Dudley mining community with me. When I look forward I realize it's just the beginning.